"Don't be afraid to share your beautiful smile."
- Pieter Van Der Westhuizen

The Significance of Being Born
8 Methods to Uncover Your Purpose

2017

Copyright © 2017
Tribute Publishing, LLC.
Frisco, Texas U.S.A

The Significance of Being Born
First Edition June, 2017

All Worldwide Rights Reserved
ISBN: 978-0-9982860-4-4

All Rights Reserved. No part of this book may be reproduced, stored in a retrieval system, or transmitted, in any form, or by any means, electronic, mechanical, recorded, photocopied, or otherwise, without the prior written permission of the copyright owner, except by a reviewer who may quote brief passages in a review.

This book is dedicated to my mom and dad who taught me what love is, and to every person who has ever felt lost or worthless.

Remember that Jesus loves you!

Contents

Foreword xi

Chapter 1 – How Were You Created? 1

Chapter 2 – Finding Your Place 11

Chapter 3 – The Essence of Humanity 21

Chapter 4 – The Importance of Love 29

Chapter 5 – How to Deal with Rejection 37

Chapter 6 – Determine Your Purpose 43

Chapter 7 – The Importance of Positivity 57

Chapter 8 – Connecting with God 67

Chapter 9 – The Significance of Reward 79

Chapter 10 – Living a Significant Life 87

About the Author 105

x

Foreword

Why are you here? Why were you born? Why have you been given the life you are living? What is the purpose of your life? These are just a few questions that every human on the planet has asked themselves at one point in time.

We have all struggled with finding purpose in a world where it seems that people have forgotten about the key aspect of being human. Humanity!

What is humanity? The Webster's dictionary defines humanity as the quality or state of being humane. Humane, in turn, is defined as being marked by compassion, sympathy, or consideration for humans or animals. The thing that sets us apart then, and qualifies us as human beings is the ability to be kind, compassionate, caring, and considerate towards not only our fellow man, but also the animals that share this earth with us. Animals are known to show kindness to each other. They show happiness just like a dog who sees his owner when he returns home. They show remorse when they were naughty and they mourn the death of a loved one. What sets us apart from them is our higher cognitive function, our free will to choose between right and wrong, and the ability to have a relationship with God.

In Genesis 1:28, God gave humans a clear and concise mission. "Then God blessed them, and God said to them, 'Be fruitful and multiply; fill the earth and subdue it; have dominion over the fish of the sea, over the birds of the air, and over every living thing that moves on the earth.'" NKJV

We were to fill the earth, subdue it, and have dominion over all living things. The filling part was pretty much self-explanatory and we never had a problem with that. When it came to the subduing and having dominion however, that is where we are having some trouble.

To subdue something means to conquer and bring under one's control. We were commanded to subdue the earth, not animals or other humans. Dominion in turn means to have supreme authority over something. Here we were given the authority to rule over animals. Why is it that human beings have forgotten these clear guidelines and felt it relevant and right to destroy certain animals to the point of extinction, and to think that certain lives matter more than others do? In order for us to truly understand the significance of our birth, we need to find our way back to the core of who we are. Human(e) Beings!

To do this, we will be going through the entire process of life from conception to our ultimate demise. Now don't worry, this book is not about biology, but about the journey of life, and how important it is. It is about why we are here and what we need to be doing while we are here.

What does it mean to be significant? We were all created for some magnificent reason, and we all have a purpose for being placed on this earth. The reality is that there are people right now within your circle of influence that look up to you and you have a responsibility towards those people to embrace them, to teach them, and to show them who they have the ability to become. There are so many people out there in the world that feel meaningless, that feel that their life has no purpose and it saddens me, because you were created for a reason. There is no such thing as a coincidence, and you being here is no coincidence.

I look at newspapers and I get so deeply saddened by what is going on in the world today. People are dying. Some of them are taking their own lives, others are taking other people's lives. People are killing other people, especially in South Africa for insignificant things such as road rage and domestic abuse. We see people murdered daily for a cell phone or a wristwatch, something so insignificant, yet someone had to pay with their life (and don't tell me that it's poverty because it's not). Many people argue that violent robberies are because of poverty, that when people don't have anything, then they resort to stealing. I have met many people with nothing, yet they will never resort to stealing or killing. They will find a way, they will make a way, they will not murder people for a cell phone or for a ring or for earrings. When did life become so worthless that we as humans think it's okay to kill someone? It's never okay! Life is valuable life, life is precious, life is a miracle, and we cannot look at the significance of life and say how precious and amazing it is and not address the topics of abortion, murder, physical abuse, addiction, and hatred. Now I know that abortion is a difficult topic, because many people will argue that it's your choice whether you want to keep the child or not, or whether you will be able to take care of the child or not. My question is, when did we receive the power to choose over life and death of someone else? Who gave us the power of God to pick and choose who can live and die?

The fact is that a lot of young women today want to live a life of fun and excitement. When something happens and they accidentally fall pregnant, then they want to end the little child's life because it doesn't fit in to their image of what their life must be. Young men force women into having unprotected sex, then refuse to step up and take responsibility for their actions. Even worse, there are parents out there who force their children to get abortions because of the embarrassment on the family name. Seriously people, when did it become more important to look good than to actually do good? How is it okay to kill someone just to save face? I don't get it. Every single person in this world is valuable and has meaning. Now don't go telling me that when a child is not born yet, they do not have consciousness and that they are not a living being yet. From the moment that conception has taken place, within a very short space of time, there is a heartbeat. If there is a heartbeat then there's life. Neuroscience has also proven that children still carry the effects of trauma they endured during the time they were in their mother's womb. That, to me, says that there is consciousness. That child is able to feel, to understand, and to experience the emotions of the parent, of the mother. Every single child living, born or unborn, carries within him or her, their parents' DNA.

Whether you are a man or a woman, you do not have the right to choose who lives or dies because you made a mistake. If you made a mistake, it's time for you to live up to it and take responsibility and raise that child. Do your best, and if you cannot, then give him or her to somebody who can! There are millions of people in the world today who struggle to have children that would do anything to be able to have a child of their own, yet we go and decide that it's okay to kill a beautiful, sweet life, a blessing that we're given. Please remember, that every single life is significant.

There are countless stories of people that were born from a mother who didn't want them or who tried to abort them, but were either unsuccessful in the abortion attempt or were orphaned. Some of those children ended up in foster care, some of them ended up being homeless, and some of them ended up with loving families who changed their lives. The thing is, it doesn't matter where they ended up because all of them have intrinsic value. Some of those people changed the world completely. Just a few examples of these are Claire Culwell, Dr. Imre Téglásy, Brandi Lozier, Gianna Jessen, Melissa Ohden and Bishop Ron Archer. Then, there are also some people whose mothers changed their mind on aborting them just before the procedure was done, thus giving them a chance of life. Some examples of these are Celine Dion, Steve Jobs, Nick Cannon, Sher, Justin Bieber, Andrea Bocelli, Jack Nicholson and Tim Tebow.

If you can change one person's life, then life is worth it. Similarly, if a child is born today, that child throughout his or her lifespan can impact one person positively, and help that person believe in themselves, and ultimately go on to change the world. We never know the impact a person can have in this world. That is the value of being human, that is the value of having an opportunity.

Every life has value and everyone has the potential of having a profound impact on this world. We, as human beings, should not destroy life, no matter how small, since we do not know the profound destiny that God may have planned for that person. Everyone should be given the opportunity and choice to live up to their true potential.

We, as human beings, need to stop devaluing life. We need to value not only the lives of people, but of animals. We need to see life as God has made it; it's a miracle. We cannot go on living life devaluing people and going around killing people. This is not what we as humans are supposed to do. I am sickened by the level of racism in the world today. I grew up in South Africa during the Apartheid era and there are many things said about the Apartheid era, some of which are true and most of which are lies. People believe what they want to believe and they don't necessarily seek out the facts. Because of that, throughout the world today it has become apparent that some feel it's okay to discriminate in one direction, but it's completely wrong to discriminate in the other direction. How is this fair? The truth is that it's not, and we as human beings should forget about color and race and where you come from. The fact is, we are all human beings. In God's eyes, we are created equal. (Genesis 1:27) His love covers all. (Romans 5:8) I don't understand why some people feel it's okay to attack someone because of skin color, black or white, because it goes both ways, and the same goes for religion. I am a Christian, I love God with all my heart, and I believe that Jesus Christ died for me. I will go on proclaiming that with all my heart for the rest of my life, but what I will not do is judge other people. Because I am not their judge. (Matthew 7:1-5)

I wasn't placed here to judge anyone and neither were you. My job as a man of God and as a believer is to love people, to care for them, and to see them in the way that Jesus sees them, so that I can plant seeds and water them and God can sprout those seeds. It's not my job to change people. That job belongs to God and the Holy Spirit. If I go around judging people, then I am doing more damage than good and that is not what we are supposed to do. Hating people because they don't believe the same things we do is wrong. That is not what we are supposed to be doing. We need to live a life that is pleasing to the Lord. (Colossians 3:17) We need to love our fellow man and woman.-We need to show them what it's like to truly have people that care for them regardless of who they are, regardless of where they came from, the color of their skin, or their beliefs, and to truly love every single human being. We need to stand together. (Colossians 3:15)

Let us look at the journey from feeling inferior to realizing your significance.

Chapter 1

How Were You Created?

In the Bible, the story is told of how God created the earth. It speaks about God speaking and matter forming instantly at His word. God said, "Let there be light," and there was light. (Genesis 1:3) All throughout the creation story, it tells how God created every living creature on the earth and in the water. When it comes to Genesis 2:7, it says "And the Lord God formed man of the dust of the ground and breathed into his nostrils the breath of life; and man became a living being." You see, here it makes specific mention of God taking physical action in making man. He formed man from the dust of the earth. If you think of how a potter makes clay pots or statuettes, then we can surmise that God mixed the dust with water. Then He used His own hands to form man into the shape He wanted. Now if we take into consideration that skin cells and sweat contains DNA, then it is safe to say that while God was creating and shaping and molding man, He was imparting His own DNA into man. This means that the first man, Adam, had the DNA of God Almighty in him, and because we are all descendants of Adam, that means that we also carry the DNA of God inside us. That means that we are all descendants from a royal bloodline, from the King of Kings.

Chapter 1 – How Were You Created?

God intended every person on this planet to play a vital role in His grand design. However, God gave us freedom of choice and He longs for us to choose Him. He does not force Himself onto us. He patiently waits like a loving father until we choose Him.

Now let us look at what modern science knows about childbirth. According to Dr. Charles Lindemann's Lab[1], a male can ejaculate between 40 million and 500 million sperm at a time. This means that you had a one in 500 million chance of being you. However, I believe that it did not happen by chance that you were the one to succeed. You were chosen by God as the right one at the right time and made it happen exactly that way. Out of a pool of 500 million possible candidates, God chose you.

"But when it pleased God, who separated me from my mother's womb and called me through His grace, to reveal His Son in me." - Galatians 1:15

Throughout this book, I will share 8 methods that you can use to discover the significance of your life. These methods, when used daily, will help you to overcome the feeling of worthlessness and help you see your value as viewed through the eyes of God.

Method 1 – Remind yourself that you were made by God!
Now that we know that you were meant to be here, let us look at the beautiful process that made you who you are. Once the egg and the sperm meet, half of the father's DNA and half of the mother's DNA join together and you are created. Cells start to split and you start getting bigger.

Chapter 1 – How Were You Created?

By week 5, you are about the size of a peppercorn and your heart, spinal cord, and facial features are beginning to form. Blood starts pumping through your veins. Even at this small stage while you still look like a tadpole, you already have a heartbeat. You are alive! By week 10, you already have almost all the anatomical features of an adult human. From week 13 onwards, all of your internal organs are formed and will keep growing as you do. At this stage, you can already start to hear and understand your mothers voice. You learn your language from your mother throughout the pregnancy. You learn certain words that you can also remember after you are born. Throughout your growth period, you learn words and you can differentiate between different voices. This is why it is important to speak empowering words to your unborn child.

By week 22 you start to kick and you are now either a boy or a girl. You are now about the size of a coconut. At about week 26 you can now taste, hear, and smell, and even your vocal cords are formed. You hear all the things that are going on inside your mother. You can feel your mother's touch. By week 28 you are opening your eyes and blinking. You are also starting to practice your breathing. You can also start to dream, which means you have a fully functioning mind. In the final weeks leading up to your birth you grow rapidly and in the last weeks can add about a pound or more per week. Your mother is now feeding you antibodies that will help you to stay healthy and to have a strong immune system. These antibodies will continue to be fed to you even after birth through your mother's breast milk, which will further strengthen your immune system. Finally, after 38 to 40 weeks, you are born into this beautiful world.

Chapter 1 – How Were You Created?

Something even more amazing about the bond between a mother and a child is that you, as an unborn child, can send stem cells to your mother's heart to repair it if it should get damaged. Male babies also leave small traces of their DNA on their mother's brain, which could help to protect the mother from brain disease such as Alzheimer's. According to IFL Science, a mother's breast milk will also be customized according to the sex of the baby.[2]

You see, the journey of life is not just an accident. It's not something that just happens. It is truly a miracle. This journey through how life is created is an extensive one. There is much more that happens during a pregnancy that I did not mention here. There is a vast number of places where you can learn about the full journey. My purpose here is to show you how significant life is. Life does not just happen. It is a grand design, set in motion by an all-knowing and loving God. There is no such thing as an accidental pregnancy. We sometimes may not plan for it to happen, but God has a purpose with every life.

If God went through this entire purpose of creating you, then you are truly worthwhile and have a purpose. If we look at the beauty of DNA we can see how incredible God made us. If someone would try to type your entire genome that is within your DNA it would take them 50 years, typing 60 words per minute, working 8 hours a day, nonstop. Every single cell inside your body contains your DNA, except for red blood cells. Every cell contains a DNA chain that is about 2 meters long. Humans have about 100 trillion cells. That means that if you were to pull out your entire DNA into

Chapter 1 – How Were You Created?

a long chain, it could stretch for about 200 trillion meters. This is the equivalent to go to the sun and back more than 600 times.

Can you see that life is so amazing? It is a miracle and no matter how much people try to diminish the value of life to suit their needs, it will always be valuable. We as humans do not have the right to pick and choose which lives are more valuable than others.

God created every single one of us, and he painstakingly fashioned every single part of our bodies with his own hands. This is evident when we look at the entire period from conception to birth. That's why it is written, "I knew you before I formed you in your mother's womb," in Jeremiah 1:5, and in Psalm 139:13, "You made all the delicate, inner parts of my body and knit me together in my mother's womb. I praise you because I am fearfully and wonderfully made; Your works are wonderful, I know that well."
God formed you!

You are so incredibly special to God, and so is every other life on this planet. And as such, God expects us to value it, just as much as He does. This leads us to a whole conundrum where feminists are trying to say that there is no life in the womb, and that every woman should be entitled to choose to abort her child at any stage before birth, right up until full term.

Now let me get something clear, I am not a mother, nor will I ever be a mother. I believe that mothers are handpicked by

Chapter 1 – How Were You Created?

God Himself to fulfill a task that only a woman can perform. A mother can nurture and love and has the ability to give of her own life force while supporting life inside of her. Women around the world are trying so hard to be like men, when, in my opinion, women are in some instances more unique than men are. Women are more intuitive, more beautiful, more caring, better at nurturing, and have the ability to calm down even the fiercest warrior, when that warrior is her soulmate. Women were not made to be the same as men. Women were made to support men, not as an inferior being, but as part of the man. (Ephesians 5:22-23; Colossians 3:18) That's why a woman was made from the rib of a man, (Genesis 2:23) not because God wasn't able to make women without the rib, but because He wanted women to be internally connected to their man, just as the rib is a vital part of protecting the heart. You see, women, you are special, you are close to your man's heart, and you play a vital role in keeping his heart safe. It is also vital for every woman to understand that throughout history, there were many amazing influencers in the world, people that changed the course of history… great people. But not even one of those people would have ever been able to exist if it was not for a mother and a father. I have heard many acceptance speeches after someone received a trophy, or medal, or prize, and more often than not, the mother is the one being honored in that speech. Be proud of who you are! You are exceptional, you are the incubators of humanity and without you, there would be no humanity.

With regard to when life exists in the womb, it is important to look at Proverbs 23:22. It says "Listen to your father, who gave you life, and don't despise your mother when she is

Chapter 1 – How Were You Created?

old." In this verse, it is clear that life was given by the father and from the conception process you read earlier, it is clear to understand. An egg from a woman is just an egg and will not turn into a baby without being implanted by the sperm from the father. Once this implantation has occurred, then the miracle of life starts to spring forth inside the womb. Immediately after implantation occurs, then there is life.

I believe that most of us have, at some point or another, seen someone lying in a hospital bed connected to all the machines, if not in person, then in a movie or TV show. One of all the many machines is the heart rate monitor, and when life slips away, we can hear the telltale sign of the continuous high pitched beep signifying that there is no longer a heartbeat. If the absence of a heart beat signifies death, then should it not also be the determining factor of life? When there is a heartbeat, then there is life!

When we look at the old testament in the bible, we can see that not only was injuring an unborn child wrong, but it was punishable by death.

"If people are fighting and hit a pregnant woman and she gives birth prematurely but there is no serious injury, the offender must be fined whatever the woman's husband demands and the court allows. But if there is serious injury, you are to take life for life." Exodus 21:22-23

Now I am not saying that we should revert back to that practice, but what I am trying to convey is how valuable an unborn human life is. It does not matter if that life does not

Chapter 1 – How Were You Created?

conform to our image of a perfect child, but that every life is made in the image of God. (Genesis 1:27) Every life is precious and significant, so doctors, stop this selective breeding nonsense of killing every child that does not fit into society according to us.

If you are a woman reading this and you have aborted a child before, then please know that God loves you very much. He knows that people make mistakes and that we act in what we believe to be the best way at the time, but He loves you. He understands the hurt you are filled with because every life from within you not only comes from you, but also leaves a trace behind. And even though a child may have been removed, no matter how small, that child still leaves a little something behind. God is there for you! He wants to help you to bring healing to your biggest hurt. Remember that God's grace is bigger than our biggest sins. (Romans 3:23-24, 5:20, 6:14)

We need to stand up and speak for the unborn because they don't have a voice. They cannot defend themselves, so we need to do it.

Speak up for those who cannot speak for themselves, for the rights of all who are destitute. Proverbs 31:8 (NIV)

Now that you know what an incredible miracle you are, let us look at why you are here.

Chapter 2 – Finding Your Place

"Life is like being a soldier on an important mission from God. It is your destiny to fulfill this mission, but you have amnesia. Only once you have figured out your mission and complete it will you be free to go home."
- Pieter Van Der Westhuizen

Chapter 2 – Finding Your Place

Chapter 2

Finding Your Place

In order to live the life you desire, you need to stop holding onto the past and start living for your future. Remember that you cannot always determine what's going to happen to you, but you can determine your attitude towards it, and that is the most powerful thing of all.

We all come into this world in the same way. Regardless of race, religion, or skin color, we all come into the world kicking and screaming. We are removed from our only source of life support and thrust into a loud, bright world full of craziness, riches, poverty, adventure, peace, violence, and opportunity. It surely is a great big world out there. Unfortunately, where you were born does play a major role in where you might end up in life. The level of education of your parents, their level of wealth, the country you are born in, your race, and your religion all play a vital role in who you might become. This is, however, not set in stone.

Even though you were born in certain circumstances, your ultimate destination in life is greatly affected by your choices. This is a fact that many people do not want to believe and

Chapter 2 – Finding Your Place

would much rather play the blame game as to why they turned out the way they did.

The fact that some people are born into terrible circumstances can lead us to question God's purpose. We ask questions like, "Why are there people that would do anything to be parents and would be incredible parents, yet they can't have kids?" They are simply not physically able to have children no matter how hard they try. At the same time, we see people that are so absolutely ill-equipped to be parents. People that should have no business being parents that seem to pop out children like they are rabbits. This goes against all rationality. We question God as to why He would give these people children and not to someone that would make better parents.

The truth is that we will never understand God's thinking. What I can tell you is what I learned through my experience when I started to get involved with foster care. There are millions of people out there who, in society's eyes, should not be parents. These people are hurt and broken individuals. Because they are so hurt and broken, they struggle to handle the basic tasks and actions that other people do so easily. It is very difficult to show love when you were never given love. You cannot show skills and habits that were never modeled to you. You see, people can only do what they know, and when you know better, you do better. Because so many people simply don't know any better, they default back to what has been modeled to them their entire lives.

Chapter 2 – Finding Your Place

I have also seen how these foster children who are in the system simply crave love and acceptance. They just want to feel like they belong somewhere and that they are worthy to be loved. Their emotions are a two-edged sword and even though they may have a huge want to be and feel loved, they always feel like they do not deserve it and will rebel against those that try to love them in fear of getting hurt. This, in turn, causes pain in those that are trying to love them, and in many cases, they pull back and slowly start taking away their love, which in turn justifies the child's feeling of not being worthy of love. The only way to begin to overcome this is to keep showering them with love and approval and making them feel that they are better than they believe. Over time, (sometimes lots of time) they will slowly start to believe it, and so begins the process of healing.

I can tell you that fostering is a very difficult and trying experience, but it is also a very fulfilling one. Perhaps God wants us as humanity to step up and move out of our own selfish desires to take these lost children and help them. Perhaps that is why he does not allow some people to have their own children, because He wants them to take another child that might be lost otherwise. Perhaps God wants us to love our fellow human beings so much that we will not allow anyone to be left behind. The truth is we don't know Gods plans, and we don't have all the answers, but we need to stop questioning and start loving with no strings attached.

Let me tell you a little bit about our experience. When we started our journey, we knew it was going to be hard. We knew that we were going into the process never knowing

Chapter 2 – Finding Your Place

how long we would have a child in our lives. We started it never knowing who we will be getting or how they will change our lives. Through a lot of prayer and soul-searching, we came to the realization that many people that have their own children never know how long they will have their children in their lives. We realized that if we could make a difference in someone's life, even if it was just for a little while, then it was worth it.

He came into our lives faster than a rocket ship launched from Cape Canaveral. In an instant, our lives were different. He was so small, and so frail, and we could see the fear, pain, and confusion behind the brave face he put on. I promised myself that I would be there for him and teach him that there are good people in this world that truly care for him and others like him. I will never be able to fathom what he must have gone through, nor will I be able to feel the pain of being ripped out of the only world I know and being placed in a strange new place with new people.

I know that I have already taught him a lot and he amazes me every day at how smart he is and how quickly he learns and grows. His passion and love and caring heart inspires me every day. I am astounded by his resilience. In the beginning, I could see how confusing it all was for him, but he just kept going like a brave soldier. I hope that one day I will have his strength. He teaches me daily that life is a gift, and that we should have fun and spend time together. I have learned that I should pursue time with my family more than the allure of money or things.

Chapter 2 – Finding Your Place

Initially, I would tell people that he was my foster child and explain his situation. Now I realize my folly. For he is not my foster child. He may not have come from my seed, but God definitely gave him to us. He is so deeply imbedded into my heart that I cannot imagine being without him. He is my son, and I love him more than words could ever explain. I will always be there for him, no matter where he ends up. For now, he is with us, and we pray that it will remain that way. But God knows the plans He has for his life. And as long as we are part of that plan, I will do my best to live up to God's expectation of a good father for him.

When we started our foster care journey with him, I thought that I could be a hero to him and be there to heal his broken heart. Now, I realize that he is also a hero to me. By the way, he lives every day to his fullest, doing his best in everything and showing love to everyone. His courage inspires me daily. I love him so much.

Method 2 – Focus on glorifying God through your actions
It doesn't matter who they are or where they come from, every person and especially every child, needs love.

I can also tell you that where you come from and who you are born through does not determine who you are. In the beautiful poem *On Children* by Khalil Gibran, he writes about children saying, "They come through you but not from you." That is because you are created by the almighty God. Your parents were merely a vessel for you to be physically made manifest into this world. Because of this, your outcome is highly dependent on you and the choices you make.

Chapter 2 – Finding Your Place

Let me put it to you in the form of a story. Let us imagine that there are two very good friends. They were both born in the same hospital, they live in the same suburb, they go to the same school, and their families are of equal level of wealth. They spend almost all their time together and are inseparable. Let us call one Jim and the other John. Jim and John started playing football at a very young age. They were pretty good at it as well. Because of their athletic prowess, they inevitably become very popular. As the two boys reached high school, their football skills just kept getting better, and with that, their popularity increased. Everybody wanted to be their friends.

They both start getting involved with some friends that were not so good for them. They get involved with alcohol and tobacco, and pretty soon get the opportunity to try harder drugs. As they get more consumed by their drinking habits, they also start becoming self-absorbed and start looking down on other students. This leads to bullying. One night, as they are drinking and having a party after winning another big game, they encounter another student with less athletic ability and they start making fun of him. It quickly escalates into physical abuse. This night, however, Jim starts to feel guilty about picking on the other student and he ends the abuse. Everybody laughs at Jim and calls him a softy. Jim is upset about the name-calling, but feels worse about the abuse they have been causing to other students over the past years.

That night Jim decides to walk home instead of driving with the other guys. As he is walking and thinking about all the

Chapter 2 – Finding Your Place

bad things he has done so far in his life, he decides that he wants to change and be a better person. That night, Jim decides that he was going to put more effort into his academic and football career.

As Jim starts focusing more and more on his new conquests, John starts realizing that Jim seems different. John ask Jim why he is changing. He accuses Jim of thinking that he is better than he is. Jim assures John that he does not think so, and that he is just trying to work harder in the hope of getting a scholarship.

Eventually, as time goes on, the two best friends start to drift apart, not because either of them wanted to, but because their focus changed, and both boys were focusing on different goals.

Jim eventually ended up playing football for a huge team in the big leagues after completing his degree at a high-end university with a full scholarship. He got married, had children, moved into a high-end neighborhood, and he sent his kids to Ivy League schools. Jim was very happy. He worked hard and focused on being the best husband he could be for his wife and father to his kids. He learned how to invest well and how to build successful businesses. Jim knows that his children will have the opportunities in life that he had to work very hard to achieve.

John also graduated from high school, barely, and managed to find a college that offered him a scholarship based on his football skills. John kept in touch with a lot of his high school

Chapter 2 – Finding Your Place

buddies and would go out and party many nights. John eventually lost his scholarship due to his drinking habits, not performing academically, and not showing up for practice. He dropped out of college without a degree and without making it to the big leagues.

You see Jim and John had the same opportunities available to both of them. They both chose different paths though, and ended up in completely different places later in their lives.

Even though this story might be fictional, I believe that everyone knows a similar story, of how two people from seemingly exact backgrounds turned out completely different. This is because of the choices they made. In the same way, you can decide where you want to end up in the future. You may have been born in poverty or on the wrong side of the tracks, but that does not need to become your identity. In the first chapter, we already established that you are a miracle and that you are significant. Now you need to find your reason for being here. You need to find your place.

"Life is like being a soldier on an important mission from God. It is your destiny to fulfill this mission, but you have amnesia. Only once you have figured out your mission and complete it will you be free to go home."
Pieter Van Der Westhuizen

When you look at your life, no matter where in your life you are right now, there must be something that has given you joy and a profound sense of purpose and satisfaction.

Chapter 2 – Finding Your Place

For each person, this is different and many times might require a lot of soul searching to uncover. Once you find that thing that brings you purpose, then find a way to pursue it. Remember that we are here to glorify God and it is OK to enjoy what you do. God would never expect you to be miserable all the time. He wants you to live a life of fulfillment and happiness while glorifying Him. Find a way to glorify God, have fun, and earn money for doing what you love. If it is your job, then that is OK, as long as you find a way to live God's purpose for your life in your chosen career. When you figure out how to do this, then you are on your way to finding true happiness within your purpose. Being successful at something, however, is not enough. Once you have figured out how to pursue what brings joy to your soul and make a living from it, then find a way to teach that skill to someone else. You see, we humans are always afraid of teaching someone else the skills we know due to the fear of being replaced or becoming obsolete. The truth is that by teaching someone else the skills we have mastered, we live on in them and we leave something precious behind. I believe that this is the ultimate goal of life, and that is to make a difference in the world. We do not need to end poverty, or end world hunger, or save the planet. Those are all very admirable goals, but by making a difference in one person's life, we inevitably change the world and all those other big problems can be tackled together.

Life was meant to be lived, enjoyed, experienced, and loved. It is not meant to be a drag. Find someone that you can pour into and help them to rise into the person they have the potential of being. Always see people as better than they are and help them to see it, too.

Chapter 2 – Finding Your Place

It is impossible to uplift someone else without uplifting yourself as well, and that gives great meaning to life. When you see someone else rising from ruins making a difference not only in their own and their families lives, but also in their community, that is worth living for. Don't just strive to change your life, strive to change the world by changing one person at a time!

Chapter 3

The Essence of Humanity

Humanity. It has come to mean a collective of humans from all around the world. A species with a higher form of intelligence. The word goes hand in hand with the word humane, which means kindness or benevolence. If we take this in consideration, then we as human beings need to be kind to one another and treat each other with love and respect. (John 13:34) When we look at history, however, this could not be further from the truth.

You see, throughout history there are countless stories of horrible atrocities done to our fellow human beings around the world. The genocide that was committed in America against the Native American Indians, the Aborigines in Australia, the Tutsi tribe in Rwanda, and the Jews in Nazi Germany are just a few examples of these atrocities. Many atrocities are committed by so-called first world countries. These acts are so cruel and disturbing that one can hardly believe that one human could treat another human that way. And yet, even today these things are still occurring all over the world. Just look at what is happening right now to the people in Syria. It saddens me to see how people are tortured and killed every single day across the world. I live in a small

Chapter 3 – The Essence of Humanity

town in South Africa, and every week in our local newspaper there are at least three cases of murder in our little community. Just yesterday, I read about a 9-year-old girl who had to watch as her mother and grandfather were beaten to death with a shovel over a wage dispute, and when she ran away, she was chased down and murdered by the same men. In Nigeria, people are being publicly beaten and tortured and set on fire while still alive. The world has become so distorted that people would rather stand by and take a video on their cellphones than do something about it.

If we allow this type of action towards our fellow human beings, then how can we call ourselves human at all? Every day I see how people are being attacked emotionally and physically because of the color of their skin or their spiritual beliefs. Social media has created a lot of armchair terrorists that spend all of their time attacking others for their beliefs and actions, yet those same people never have the guts to stand up for anything in life. People care more about how many followers they have on Twitter or Instagram or how many Facebook friends they have than how they care for their fellow human beings.

Charles Frederic Aked quoted, "For evil men to accomplish their purpose, it is only necessary that good men do nothing."

We need to stand up and fight against what is wrong. Every day more and more people are being attacked because of quoting a Scripture or praying in public or thanking God in

Chapter 3 – The Essence of Humanity

a victory speech. Yet, serious acts of violence and genocide are overlooked because of who is committing these crimes. Two wrongs do not make a right. We cannot make the world a better place by repaying evil with evil. How can we rise above our savage history if we refuse to leave it in the past? I remember a beautiful story from my childhood. The story is about how a loving God created the entire world and all living creatures upon it. He created Adam, the first man, and Eve, the first woman. If we look at this, then that means that we are all descendants of Adam and Eve, hence, we are all family. Now we all know that it is quite common for every family to have a fight now and then, get mad at each other, and even stay mad for a long time. However, as with Cain and Abel, who were two brothers, it is never OK to kill. Now, there is no denying that we, as humans, are falling short big time! When it comes to loving our neighbors as we love ourselves, we lose the plot.

So, what can we do to change that? What can we do to shake off the evils of our past and rise above our differences to a place where we can all live together in harmony? Let me start with a tale of a very rich man who decided that he wanted to take his 8-year-old son on an African safari. When they went on the safari, they saw all the amazing animals and the amazing beauty of the African plains. They finally reached a village where the young boy got to play with some of the local children. One of the children could speak English and so they were able to communicate and learn about each other's lives and cultures as they played. The rich boy noticed that these African children didn't dress like him. Their clothes were different, and they were dirty from playing

Chapter 3 – The Essence of Humanity

outside the whole day. They were carefree and played everywhere their hearts desired, and they knew the bush and the different types of animals very well. The boys really enjoyed playing together and had an incredible time. That night, the rich boy told his father about all the things he learned that day. He felt sad that they did not have electricity or TV or internet. They didn't have nice clothes and fancy shoes. He decided that he would like to help them in some way and resolved to ask his new friend the next day as to what he could do. When he asked his friend what he could do to help them live a better life, his friend's reply surprised him. His friend said that they didn't care not having all those things, and that they actually preferred it that way. You see, this tribe tried to hang onto their historic roots and did not want to lose their proud history through the introduction of technology. They loved to be so completely intertwined with nature that it was a part of them. They did not want to be surrounded by high brick walls and spend their playtime behind a TV screen.

You see, when we look at other people's situation from our perspective, then it might look like they have lack and that they are suffering because they do not have what we have. But, when we look at things through their eyes, then the picture changes completely. We are too quick to call fowl these days, even before we have all the facts. We see a man with a backpack walking along the road and we think, shame, the poor man, he must be homeless. When in fact, the man is walking across the continent to raise money for cancer research because he lost his wife to cancer recently.

Chapter 3 – The Essence of Humanity

We see a Muslim woman wearing a hijab, and we think, shame, the poor woman, she is oppressed, when the fact is that it is part of her religion and she chooses to wear it. Now I know that there are cases where some of the women may be oppressed and where that guy might be homeless, but we should not be so quick to judge.

We need to try to understand someone's situation and conviction before we try to change it. This is only possible when we see every person out of a position of mutual respect. We need to listen to someone to truly try to understand where they come from. If we understand why a person acts a certain way, then we have better insight into how we can change the situation in such a manner as to help everyone grow through the process. By attacking a person's belief, we drive them away instead of helping them.

We need to value people, not only people that agree with our point of view, but all people. Once we start to value people, then we can start truly valuing human life, and ultimately, all life. Every single life on this planet is valuable and we should see it that way. We should fight for things of value and not some enforced ideals.

It has been proven many times through history how racial hatred was used as a weapon to create division between a local population to make them weaker and easier to invade and control. This was done by the British Empire in India and South Africa. Even today you can see how governments use racial tension to create division within the population, and while the citizens fight amongst each other the

Chapter 3 – The Essence of Humanity

government can drive their own personal agenda of increasing their power and hold onto the people. We need to learn from each other so we can grow together, regardless of race or religion.

"But love your enemies, do good to them, and lend to them without expecting to get anything back. Then your reward will be great, and you will be children of the Most High, because he is kind to the ungrateful and wicked." Luke 6:35

Remember that hatred is not inborn, it's inbred. We teach our children how to treat other people, and if they learn from our actions that it is OK to hurt, insult, attack, or humiliate someone else, then they will do it as well. Children don't learn from what you tell them, they learn through what you show them through the actions you display on a daily basis. Make sure that you are setting a good example for your children. (Proverbs 22:6)

So what is the essence of humanity?
It is to love every person on the planet as a valued part of our collective. Love them as a brother or sister, since we are truly all family. Treat each other with respect. When there is nothing kind to say, then rather not say it. Hug someone when they are feeling down or just because you can see they need a hug.

Method 3 – Focus on bringing hope to humanity.
Be a beacon of hope to those around you. Always give more smiles and compliments than you receive. Listen to someone just to hear what they have to say, without wanting to answer

Chapter 3 – The Essence of Humanity

or comment, but just to listen. Uplift them and make them believe in their dreams again.

If we treat our fellow humans in a loving manner every second of every day, then love and hope will grow across the globe and one day, hopefully, will wipe out hatred. (Matthew 5:14-16)

Make sure that you are known as the kindest person anyone knows. Help people without expecting anything back. John Bunyan said, "You have not lived today until you have done something for someone who can never repay you."

Make it a habit to sow kindness and love as seeds that will bloom into beautiful flowers for all the children of tomorrow to see!

> "Hope is the spark that will set fire to the dried-out remnants of your life!"
> - Pieter Van Der Westhuizen

Chapter 3 – The Essence of Humanity

Chapter 4

The Importance of Love

Method 4 – Love without holding back.

Love. The one word that is probably most used and misused in the world today. Most of us start hearing it from a very young age. We hear people using it to describe the way they feel about fries or ice cream. We hear how young girls are so madly in love with a boy they barely know. The fact is that we as humanity, in many cases, have forgotten the true meaning of love.

One of the most popular Scriptures about love that you almost certainly heard before at a wedding is 1 Corinthians 13:4-8, which goes as follows: "Love is patient, love is kind. It does not envy, it does not boast, it is not proud. It does not dishonor others, it is not self-seeking, it is not easily angered, it keeps no record of wrongs. Love does not delight in evil but rejoices with the truth. It always protects, always trusts, always hopes, always perseveres. Love never fails."

To truly understand the significance and power of this Scripture, we need to look at it one section at a time.

Let us start with "Love is patient."

Chapter 4 – The Importance of Love

According to dictionary.com patience is defined as the quality of being patient as the bearing of provocation, annoyance, misfortune, or pain without complaint, loss of temper, irritation, or the like, and an ability or willingness to suppress restlessness or annoyance when confronted with delay.

This means that even when things are not working out the way we would like, we can still be calm and reasonable in handling a situation. Staying calm when someone is driving slower than the speed limit is patience. Respecting someone's personal space when they take a little bit longer to leave the cash register after paying when they are in front of you is patience. Understanding that people learn at different rates and their level of hearing may differ and to not get annoyed when they ask the same question more than once, is patience. Not snapping at your husband or wife if they don't do things exactly the way you want it done is patience. Being patient means that you are willing to let other people do things at their own rate regardless of how it affects you at that point.

Now let's take a look at "Love is kind."

Kindness is the act of how you treat other people or animals. Kindness is understanding that other people have feelings too, and that the way you treat them will have an effect on them not only for that day, but maybe even their entire life. I still remember how a hurtful word that some random kid called me when I was 4 years old affected the way I saw myself well into adulthood. We may not always realize it, but our words and actions are far more powerful than we think. That is why it is so important to always be kind.

Chapter 4 – The Importance of Love

"It does not envy"

We have all been caught by this little green monster. Envy or jealousy is when we can't be happy for someone else. We get upset when someone else receives something we have been wanting for a long time. When someone else gets a promotion or has business success, we get upset because we didn't get it. When a friend or family member buys a new car, we get upset because we don't have a new car. We don't even want the same car, but we are just upset because they got one and we didn't.

We need to start to be happy for others when they are blessed. Stop being envious and judging others for their successes, and be happy for them. Then you are walking in love.

"It does not boast"

Hand in hand with the above section of envy, you should not boast about your great fortune to others as well. There is nothing wrong with being proud of your achievements and successes, but when you deliberately throw it in someone else's face, then you are no longer acting from a position of love, but rather trying to show them that you are better than them. This will, in turn, cause them to resent you and your successes and they will struggle to find success, and you played a role in that.

Jesus shared a story in the bible of a rich man whose fields produced such a large harvest that he did not have enough storage for it all. The man boasted in himself and his successes and said that he would tear down his storage, build bigger ones, and that he would rest and be merry and drink

Chapter 4 – The Importance of Love

wine. The story tells us how, because of his foolish ways, his life was taken from him. You see, the fact is that his blessings and successes were a gift from God, and by him boasting in himself he took the glory away from God. We need to always be thankful, and when we have abundance, we should be willing to share it. Support others and help them to achieve what you did, and lift them up to be better.

"Love is not proud"

Being proud can mean that you are too proud to accept help from someone else. You trust only in yourself and you think that no one else can do the job as good as you can. In business terms, it is someone who cannot delegate tasks to someone else, or when they do, they micro manage every aspect of how they do the job. We need to trust others and not be afraid to say that we need help.

In 2 Corinthians 12:9 Paul said this, "And He said to me, 'My grace is sufficient for you, for My strength is made perfect in weakness.' Therefore, most gladly I will rather boast in my infirmities, that the power of Christ may rest upon me."

We need to boast in the power of God. When we are weak, He can show His strength and power through the miracles he does in our lives. When things happen that bring breakthrough in your life you can't explain, that is God at work in your life. Do not boast or be proud in and of yourself, but boast about God's greatness.

"It does not dishonor others"

When you walk in love, you do not humiliate others. You do not laugh at them or mock them or disgrace them. You treat them with kindness and love. For example, if you see someone with toothpaste on their cheek or something stuck in their teeth, instead of calling them out and making a joke of it, simply pull them aside and discreetly tell them, to spare them embarrassment. Do not delight yourself in someone else's misfortune.

"It is not self-seeking"

In today's world, we see that people care so much about how popular they are or how many followers and friends they have on social media. We see girls wearing skimpy outfits and doing ridiculous things on webcams. And there's the selfie obsession. People are so obsessed about having a following that they would do just about anything to gain popularity. People are hurting themselves or others just so they will get more likes. We need to stop focusing just on ourselves and our own vanity and focus on loving and helping others.

"It is not easily angered"

People seem to get angry so easily these days. Road rage is rampant and some will even kill a fellow human being simply because they cut them off in traffic. Seriously, has life become so devalued that we think it's OK to kill someone just because of a minor inconvenience? Women snap because their husband's leave the toilet seat up, and husbands because their wives may have scratched the car. We get upset by the silliest things, and many times, this leads to bigger problems. In South Africa, we have seen how one man got angry about a taxi cutting him off in traffic lead to a riot and an almost-movie-like taxi war, with bullets flying everywhere and innocent people being injured. We need to

Chapter 4 – The Importance of Love

learn to handle our tempers much better, and keep calm when something is trying to upset us.

"It keeps no record of wrongs"

Here I believe that women are experts, but men can also be pretty good at it. We say that we are walking in love, but when the next fight about something silly occurs, then all the old issues are dug up. Something that happened months or even years earlier are drawn right back into the fight. We need to forgive and forget. I have heard many people say, "I will forgive, but never forget." This is the wrong attitude. It is true that it is difficult to forget when someone has hurt you, but forgiveness means forgetting. You cannot truly forgive if you constantly keep dragging the issue back up. When you commit to forget about it, then you can start the healing process that comes with true forgiveness. We cannot keep blaming people for slavery or apartheid when most of the people living today were not even directly impacted by it. If we truly want to move on, we need to forget about it and move forward, not backwards or in reverse by repaying a wrong with another wrong. Forget about the wrongs and choose to remain and walk in love.

"Love does not delight in evil but rejoices with the truth"

There is a saying that says the truth will set you free. This means that when you are constantly telling and living in the truth, then you have nothing to hide. You can be free to be joyful knowing that you will never be caught telling a lie. We need to love people enough to tell them the truth, but in a loving manner. Do not keep quiet when you see something wrong, speak up. But speaking up does not mean you have

Chapter 4 – The Importance of Love

to attack. I once had a boss that always said, "Don't come to me with a problem if you can't bring a solution with it." I believe that this is a good philosophy to have. When you want to point out a problem, then bring a solution with it.

"It always protects, always trusts, always hopes, always perseveres"

Love means protecting that which is important to you, trusting that others have your best interest at heart, and you, theirs. Love means hoping in a better future and preserving that which is important to you. When we truly walk in love, it encompasses all of these things and more. We cannot pick and choose which of these aspects we want to use and adhere to. We need to embrace love in its entire splendor.

"Love never fails"

When we embrace love in its fullness, then we can grow as a species to become what we are truly capable of becoming. We can focus on saving the planet, ending world hunger and ending genocide and corruption and oppression across the globe. We can focus on finding solutions while constantly walking in love.

"And now these three remain: faith, hope and love. But the greatest of these is love." 1 Corinthians 13:13

Love is the greatest weapon we have to fight against all the wrongs in the world. If we truly want to change the world, we need to start walking in love and value every single life in the knowledge of how significant it is.

"Dear friends, let us love one another, for love comes from God. Everyone who loves has been born of God and knows

Chapter 4 – The Importance of Love

God. But anyone who does not love does not know God, for God is love." 1 John 4:7-8

Do you see how important it is for us to love one another? We are all created by a loving God, who loved us so much that He sent His Son Jesus Christ to die for each and every one of us so we can be saved. (Romans 5:8) According to 1 John 4:8, "He who does not love does not know God, for God is love." For this reason, because God is love, we should strive to constantly walk in love toward our fellow human beings.

Chapter 5

How to Deal with Rejection

Because we all have a deep longing to feel loved and accepted by other people, it can be very hurtful when we feel rejected by someone.

Rejection is probably the most feared thing in the world today.

We are all afraid of being rejected at some point of our lives. Almost every fear, when it comes to human interaction, stems from the fear of rejection. Even the number one fear of all time, the fear of public speaking, stems from the fear of being rejected by those people listening to you. We focus so much on what other people might think or say that we allow our fear to stop us from acting at all. Some people handle rejection better than others. The reason for this may come in many shapes and sizes, but ultimately the core of it all is that those who handle rejection better, have managed to find a way to not internalize what was said or done to them. They do not accept it as who they are and can move on without the words or actions becoming part of their identity.

Chapter 5 – How to Deal with Rejection

Feeling rejected is a very powerful emotion, and this becomes even more powerful and dangerous when we internalize rejection to such a point that we start rejecting ourselves. When we start to reject ourselves through our words and our actions, we are in danger of getting stuck in a downward spiral that will ultimately lead to your demise. The only way to get out of such a self-destructive pattern is to start changing your self-talk and to stop rejecting yourself. You also need to learn how to deal with rejection better.

Here are a few methods that I have learned through the last couple of years that have greatly helped me.

The first method to dealing with rejection may sound silly, but it can be a very powerful method. When someone insults you or attacks you verbally, instead of trying to defend yourself, simply look them in the eyes and say, "Thank you for sharing." These four words are so powerful in dealing with someone who is trying to insult you because it shows them that you are confident, in charge of your emotions, and that you refuse to accept it.

You see, many times when people insult you, it is because they are trying to get a reaction from you. They want you to get upset and try to fight back and protect yourself. While you are in an emotional state, you oftentimes say the wrong things and allow what they said to get under your skin. Once this happens, it becomes more difficult to get rid of it. By simply not allowing their words inside your mind and refusing to let it become part of you, you disarm them and you maintain the power.

Chapter 5 – How to Deal with Rejection

Think of your emotions, and anger in particular, as a nuclear missile. You should not allow the launch button of your emotional nuclear missile to be placed in the hands of anyone else. That is why you need to always maintain control of your launch controls. Never try to justify or fight back. Stay in control.

The second method is in acting like you did not hear them. By saying that you did not hear them, you are, in essence, telling them to repeat what they said. By doing this, many times people will have to rethink about what they said. This second thought over of their words might cause them to rethink what they said. Many people, including myself, will suffer from foot-in-mouth disease, which means that they will say things without thinking it through. Once a person has the opportunity to rethink what they said, they realize that it can be hurtful and will refrain from saying it. Of course, you always get some miserable people that are trying to get a reaction from you and will repeat their statement again. This will then lead to the third method of dealing with them.

Ask them directly if they are trying to hurt your feelings. For most people, this will cause them to relook at what they said and they may find a better way of getting their point across without hurting your feelings. I believe that most people will not willingly hurt your feelings and this step will help clarify their intentions. There are, however, a rare few wretched individuals who deliberately want to hurt your feelings and will say so. Your defense against people like this is step number four.

Simply tell them, "I refuse to accept that."

Chapter 5 – How to Deal with Rejection

Let me explain in the form of a story.

There was once a father who had a son very late in his life. When he was fifty years old, his son was five. Even though the father was not the age of most of the other fathers of five-year olds, he loved his son very much. He was very fit and active and spent a lot of time with his son. One day, the father took his son to the playground. Once they were there, another particularly obnoxious man constantly made hurtful remarks towards the boy's father and other people at the playground. This continued for a while and the father just smiled at the man without saying anything in return. Eventually, the man left leaving the other people in peace. The young boy came to his father and asked "Daddy, why didn't you say anything to the man? He was so mean and said so many hurtful things. Why didn't you do something?"

The father looked at his son and he said "Son, there are many people in the world who are hurting. They are so full of hate and anger that they cannot keep it in. They are like an overflowing cup. There is no room inside the cup anymore so it starts to overflow to everyone else who is close to them. If I refuse to accept what the man says, then his words belong to him. He has enough pain inside him and does not need me to add to his cup."

The son looked at his father with great love as he realized that his father was a great man.

When this father refused to take the hurtful words, he made sure that his own cup was kept free of this man's contamination. He had the power to let it into his cup, or to refuse it. By refusing to let it in, he kept control of his launch

Chapter 5 – How to Deal with Rejection

button. Also, by not responding to the man and not repaying his insults with insults, he did not add to the hurting man's cup of pain.

Make a conscious choice of not accepting insults from anyone. By understanding that people's mouths are a vessel that carries what flows from their hearts, you get to realize that what they are saying doesn't really have anything to do with you and it's got everything to do with their own hurt and pain. (Luke 6:45)

If someone still keeps insulting you after you have told them that you refuse to accept it, then as a last resort you can use step five.

By directly telling them that you understand that their words are flowing from their own hurt and do not really have anything to do with you, you are causing them to do some self-reflection. They are forced to look at themselves and evaluate where their hurt came from. Once you have said this, walk away. You no longer have anything more to say to them and whatever will be said after this is irrelevant. Always stay in control of your emotions and never allow someone else to get control of your launch button. By refusing to let anyone's insults or bad comments into your mind, you maintain control of your own subconscious mind.

Now that we have established how to handle harsh words, we can look at how to repair the hurt from the past. You need to understand that the person you believe you are because of your hurtful past is not who you are. You are incredible, you are God's creation, and you are significant.

Chapter 5 – How to Deal with Rejection

You are good enough to achieve anything you set your mind to. You are worthy to be loved, and you are worthy to be successful. Be kind to yourself, and remember that rejection is not a reflection of you, just as failure is not a reflection of you, it is merely an event that happened with a lesson that it had to teach you. Learn the lessons, but never internalize the event as part of who you are. Remember that even though rejection may feel very personal in some cases, the fact is that is rarely the case. Rejection has more to do about the other person than it has to do with you.

If you are in sales, for example, and you discuss your product with a prospect, the fact that the prospect says no to your offer has nothing to do with you. It might be that your product is just not right for them. It might not be the right time for them, or maybe they already have what you are trying to offer. More often than not, the rejection is not personal, so don't take it that way.

The most difficult rejection to deal with is when it comes from a prospective friend or life partner. Dating can be very brutal if you internalize every rejection. It is very important to understand that if one man or woman rejects you, it does not mean that the entire human race has rejected you. Your perfect match is out there, and see every 'no' as a step closer to finding that perfect partner or friend.

Be like a duck. No, not the part about sticking your head under the water, but the part where the water beads up and rolls off its feathers with ease. Let the rejection roll off you with ease, and never let it stick.

Remember, you are awesome!

Chapter 6

Determine Your Purpose

Purpose. Almost every single person in the world has, at one point in their lifetime, struggled with the question of what their purpose was, why they were here, and what they were supposed to be doing. We ask ourselves questions like, why was I even born, why was I born in this era and not another, why does he or she have to be my mother or father, and why was I born in this country?

You see, all of these questions all point to our situation and our surroundings, but the true question in reality should be, "What should I be doing with my life?" Finding answers to life's difficult questions lies in asking the right questions in the first place. Instead of asking, "Why am I here?" you can ask, "What am I supposed to be doing while I am here?" The first question has infinite possibilities and leaves you feeling overwhelmed. The second has embedded within it a call to action. By realizing that there are certain actions that you can take to lead you to your ultimate purpose, it leaves you with a sense of hope.

You see, hope is the spark that will set fire to the dried-out remnants of your life. When you are a child, you most likely

Chapter 6 – Determine Your Purpose

dream of being someone or something great. When you are between two and six years old, you are filled with wonder and hope for the future. You are positive that you are the fastest kid on the planet and nobody can keep up with you. I see it daily in my five-year-old. He is so passionate and positive. He is unstoppable! Ok, maybe only until a bee flies close by him, then he freaks out and loses it a little. It doesn't matter though, because within a few minutes, once he has calmed down, then he is king of the world again. Most of us, when we were children, were the same way. Nothing could hold us back, and nothing seemed impossible.

Somewhere during our childhood, we lose this. This can be a result of many things, but it all stems back to the same thing. We stop believing in ourselves because of a waning self-esteem. When we start losing self-esteem because of something someone said or did towards us, we start on a downhill spiral that can be very difficult to get out of, even when we become adults. We drag the baggage with us through life on a sled larger than Santa's, except we don't have flying reindeer to help us. No wonder we are constantly tired.

If we want to get back that fire we had in our soul when we were small children, we need to learn how to get rid of the baggage one bag at a time and start building our self-esteem to the level where we can sing the Barney song at the top of our lungs in a crowded shopping mall like a four-year-old would. Ok, maybe singing may not be your thing, but you get the point. You need to learn to build your confidence to

Chapter 6 – Determine Your Purpose

shake your inhibitions to chase your dreams to find your purpose.

You see, finding your purpose is not a magic tap of your heels or snap of your fingers when you instantaneously know exactly what you want to do with your life. It is a process of discovery. It is a challenge, a journey and no one can walk the journey on your behalf. You need to do it yourself.

Method 5 – Stop negative self-talk
The first thing you need to do to start building self-esteem is to use positive self-talk. I covered this in the chapter on love. The key is to stop talking negatively about yourself. Stop being your worst critic. If you spoke to your best friend the way that you speak to yourself, then you wouldn't have a best friend for very long.

Let's do this as an activity. Find a nice quiet place where you can sit and be alone, preferably someplace where someone else can't hear you. Why? Because it might get weird. Now that you have found your place, close your eyes and pretend that your best friend or loved one is standing right in front of you. It has to be a person that you truly love and respect. Now that you can clearly see the person you chose in front of you, I want you to imagine saying all the insulting words you usually say to yourself to them. Try to say it out loud while looking them straight in the eye.
Did you do it? Not so easy, is it?
The fact is that when you truly love and respect someone, then it is very difficult to insult them right to their face. It should feel uncomfortable because it is not good behavior to

Chapter 6 – Determine Your Purpose

insult other people or yourself. You understand that those words will hurt their feelings and will cause them to pull away from you, and you don't want that. Now that you understand that you don't want to say mean and hurtful things to your friends, do you also understand the damage it does to you and your own self-esteem if you speak those words to yourself? You need to stop the negative self-talk and replace it with positive self-talk.

You can start small by giving yourself one sincere compliment every morning and refusing to keep talking negatively to yourself. Once you catch yourself thinking a negative thought or saying it out loud, stop immediately and give yourself another sincere compliment. The more you do this, the easier it will get to refrain from the bad and increase the good.

Next, start to celebrate your victories, no matter how small. By celebrating those victories, you are telling yourself that it is good to have accomplishments and that you are proud of it. Now that you know how to celebrate your victories and have stopped bad-mouthing yourself, it is time to let go of some of the baggage that you have been dragging with you. It is also good to sit in a quiet space for this where you will not be disturbed. Something I like to do is close my eyes, and one by one, start bringing up the events that caused me pain. I do this one at a time and don't move on to the next event until I have fully dealt with the first one. I bring that event into remembrance, and when I have it vividly in my mind, I say these words: "This event was a bad time in my life. It was very tough and really hurt. Whatever happened that day was

Chapter 6 – Determine Your Purpose

not my intention. I refuse to let it have a negative impact on my life any longer. I am no longer that person, and I give myself permission to move on. It is now history and I will no longer think of it ever again. Good bye!" Then I take a deep breath and move on to the next one. This was difficult at first, as it brought up a lot of old emotions, but I kept going. Sometimes it did not work the first time. This might be the case for you, but that is OK. You just keep doing it every day, like I did, until it is gone. Now I am not saying that it will be easy, but if you want to truly live the best version of your life, you need to learn to let go of the past. Ok, now that we have dealt with the not so happy blast from the past, it is time to start focusing on what you want to achieve with your life. As I said, it is a journey.

First look at what it is that you enjoy doing. Now this can't be something destructive like drinking or gambling. It needs to be something that gives you joy and fulfillment. If it does not give you a true, deep sense of fulfillment, then keep looking.

Once you have found that thing that makes your heart smile a little bit every time you do it, it is time to brainstorm. Brainstorm, you ask? Why yes. You need to spend some time in deep thought or meditation about how you can pursue a purpose in a way that can help others while glorifying God and make a living doing it. Even if you can make a little bit of money, it will help you to keep going through the tough times. Remember that your focus is not to make money; rather it should be on making a difference and glorifying God. The money is just a reward for your persistent action

Chapter 6 – Determine Your Purpose

and to enjoy a life of meaning while you are here. Money is too small a thing to live for. Now, if you find it impossible to think of a way, then it is OK to find someone else to help you brainstorm. Now make sure that you find a co-brainstormer that will support you and not laugh at your attempts. Find yourself someone that will support you, and take it seriously.

Once you have found a method, or a glimmer of one, on how to turn your joy into purpose and making a living from it, then start taking action towards making it a reality. If you need help here as well, then it is OK to get help. What you are striving for here is not perfection, but progress. You want to focus on making small improvements every day. Pray regularly and spend time in the presence of God. The best answers will come from spending a lot of time in prayer. Once you have managed to get your system going and you are making a difference, (no matter how small), then start looking at how you can combine this with other projects, companies, charities, or nonprofit organizations to scale it up. Remember that this is not necessarily to make more money. The key here is to impact more people with it.

Why are we doing this? Because you get more by giving than taking. By making it a habit to constantly give to others, you will invariably keep building your self-esteem and become a more content person.

Life can be a very fulfilling experience if you make it a conscious decision to always do more than is expected from you. (Colossians 3:23)

Chapter 6 – Determine Your Purpose

At one of the companies that I worked for earlier in my life, I was appointed as a sales agent. I had to get new business for the company. My job basically entailed finding new clients, getting a contract set up, and then handing them off to our office staff where various people had specific roles to fulfill. My father raised me with an incredible work ethic, and that meant that if I made a promise to a company regarding the service to expect, then I would go out of my way to ensure that they would get what they had been promised. So, it came to pass that some of our office staff did not exactly care about my philosophy towards customer care and would drop the ball on numerous occasions. Invariably, I would step up and do their job to ensure that the client got what they were promised, and paid for. This upset the other office staff because, according to them, I was making them look bad. The truth was that they were doing a perfect job of that themselves. I merely did what they were supposed to do.

In South Africa, job creation has been a huge drive for many years. The government might have good intentions, but they go at it in all the wrong ways. The government will legislate companies to the point where the companies have very little power over what they are allowed to do when it comes to lazy or incompetent employees. This inevitably led to a culture of laziness and slacking off. People want a job, but they do not want to do the work. If you dare to fire such an individual, then they would run to the union, who would then demand that the employee be reinstated. If that failed, they would sometimes move to an all-out strike and sometimes even demand that the person that fired the employee be removed from the company. Sounds crazy?

Chapter 6 – Determine Your Purpose

Welcome to the distorted understanding of democracy that we call daily life in South Africa. I tell you these things not to complain about how bad the country is, but rather to illustrate to you the impact on an economy and a country where people are allowed to be lazy and damaging to a company without any repercussions. If more people are raised like I was to work hard and do more than what you are paid to do, then it will lead to a spirit of pride within a company and a country. This will inevitably lead to a more successful company and a stronger economy.

If you want to truly live an influential and significant life with purpose and direction, then you need to be the type of person that always does more than is expected from you. Always do more than you are paid for and one day, you will be paid more for what you do.

Zig Ziglar once told a beautiful story about a man who worked for the railway. One day as they were working in the hot sun, a train came by and a nice, private railway car pulled onto a siding. A man got out of the railway car and greeted one of the men who was working on the rails. They greeted each other like old friends and went into the railway car. After about an hour, both men came out and they gave each other a big hug, just like good friends would. The car left while the railway worker went back to where he had been working before. Some of the other guys enquired about the gentleman in the car, whom they recognized as the president of the railway company. The worker told the story of how they had been friends for twenty years, and that they had started working at the railway at the same time, doing the

Chapter 6 – Determine Your Purpose

same job. When the other workers asked why he was still doing the same work after twenty years while his friend was now the president of the railway company, the man gave a very profound reply. He said, "Twenty years ago when we started working for the company, I came to work for $3.50 an hour, while my friend came to work for the railroad."

You see when you work for a salary, then that is all that you focus on. You don't really care about much else as long as you get your salary. But, when you work for a company, then you focus on helping the company be successful. You will work hard, you will do your best, you will work diligently to help the company be profitable. You will do work that is not part of your job description and you will work late, even when nobody asked you to. You do that because you realize that by making sure the company is profitable, you ensure your own position in the company.

Unfortunately, so many people today don't even like the companies they work for. They will constantly gripe and complain about how the company just cares about profit, how the top management walks away with all the money, and how they never get any of it. When bonuses are paid, they get even worse. They always complain that they didn't get enough, yet they will never do more for the company than what is expected. The sad part about this is that they hate the company to the point that they don't want it to be successful, so the bosses won't get those big bonuses. What they fail to realize is that if the company is not successful, they will succeed in their dream of the bosses not getting big bonuses,

Chapter 6 – Determine Your Purpose

but they will be without a job because no company can survive if it is not making profits.

Part of finding your purpose is to always do more than what is expected from you. Find joy in your journey of discovery. You see, life is meant to be a happy experience, and by focusing on making life happier for others, you also make it happier for yourself. Never doubt the impact you can have. One person can have a major impact on a nation and even the world. Just look at the impact Mahatma Gandhi, Nelson Mandela, Muhammad Ali, Thomas Edison, or Oprah Winfrey had on the world. It was not money that helped them to make a difference; it was their ability to move people into feeling something, to believe in something, to stand up for something. This comes from who you are, not what you tell people. Yes, eloquent words can help, but if people don't believe in you, they will not follow you.

Now you might be asking yourself how this so suddenly moved from building self-esteem to leadership and the answer is that leadership is part of the logical progression of every person on this planet. We are all leaders. Some good, some not so good, some born, and some made. You might not think that you are a leader, but you are. Somewhere in your circle of influence there is a person that looks up to you, that listens to you, and that learns from you. This means that by not even trying, or not even wanting to, you have a direct impact on someone else's life. Hence, you are a leader.

Leadership is a very powerful and important role for all of us. Even though there is someone who might already be

Chapter 6 – Determine Your Purpose

looking up to you, the ultimate goal in leadership is not to gain more followers, but to serve others well.

How do we do this? Well, the fact is that you can't just wake up one morning and decide, I am going to lead a lot of people today. It doesn't work that way (even though some riots started that way), but we want to focus on making a positive impact, not a negative one. The only true way of becoming a good leader is by becoming the type of person that other people would want to follow. By focusing on building your own self-esteem and building your skills and helping others do the same, you are becoming such a person. Remember not to look at your past or your present position as the blueprint for your life to come and that there is nothing you can do to change it. Don't think that you have nothing to offer this world. We are all placed on this planet for a reason and we need to find our purpose. Remember that 'soldier with amnesia' quote from earlier in the book? This is where it becomes very relevant. By taking small steps daily to becoming a better person, you will start changing other people's lives as well.

Ultimately, we are here to serve the Lord, and there is a deep sense of enjoyment in knowing that you are doing that through loving God's people. We are all God's people. In John 21:15-17 Jesus asked Simon Peter, "Simon, do you love Me?" and when Simon Peter replied and said, "Yes Lord" Jesus told him to tend and feed His sheep. For those of you that don't know, we all are His sheep. That message to take care and feed His sheep is for all of us. We need to love, take care of, and feed our fellow human beings, and by doing so,

Chapter 6 – Determine Your Purpose

we are serving the Lord. There is no higher calling than that. You are a significant human being; you have a divine purpose. Your past is irrelevant. Your sins are forgiven, and you are in the best position of your life to start taking charge and live with passion and love while pursuing your purpose!

A Journey to Hope
By Pieter Van Der Westhuizen

An injured soul, A broken heart,
So much hurt, felt from the start.

I wish my life could have more meaning,
so I don't cry myself to sleep every evening.

Even though life can be tough,
I wish that I could know real love.

Then from the ashes of my broken past,
A glimmer of hope grew bright and vast.

You see in my time of desperation,
I found a love born from creation.
When I felt weak like everything's wrong
God's love took me and made me strong.

Now I am free from my past,
building a future and having a blast.
Where once I was broken and dirty with sin,
Thanks to Jesus my new life begins.

Chapter 6 – Determine Your Purpose

I praise you oh Lord, and give you my heart,
And never again will my life fall apart.

Though it might get tough,
And a little bit rough,
I will always hang on
To your perfect love!

Chapter 7 – The Importance of Positivity

Chapter 7

The Importance of Positivity

Throughout the world, a lot has been said about being positive. The ultimate source of positivity is the Spirit of God. We learn in the Bible of the importance of being spiritually connected to God. "The mind governed by the flesh is death, but the mind governed by the Spirit is life and peace." Romans 8:6 NIV. When we take this into account, we can see that the power of life and peace is in the Spirit. Not every spirit, however, is of God and today we see many instances of people getting involved with the wrong spirits. "Dear friends, do not believe every spirit, but test the spirits to see whether they are from God, because many false prophets have gone out into the world." 1 John 4:1 NIV. Not every spirit that you connect to will be good and that is why it is so important to spend time in the Word of God, learning more about Him, and getting a strong spiritual connection with Him. Later in this chapter, we will look at the effect your mindset and words can have on your surroundings.

Remember that God created everything in the universe. This is evident in the creation story in Genesis 1 and throughout the bible where reference is made to the stars in Job 38:31

Chapter 7 – The Importance of Positivity

and springs under the sea in Job 38:16. In Jonah 2:6 he mentions going down to the bottoms of the mountains within the sea. These are all things that science was only recently able to confirm. This proves that God created everything and the knowledge of the creation could only have been handed down from God to be made available to us by the writers of Scripture. All of creation is made up of matter, and because God created everything, then all matter is subject to His will, and is connected to God.

Scientists have discovered that matter is the substance of which all material is made. That means objects have mass. In physics, energy is a property of matter. Energy is used in science to describe how much potential a physical system has to change. It can be transferred between objects and converted in form. It cannot be created or destroyed. Humans, in many instances, have the ability to pick up on energy. Spiritual energy is the manifestation of divine, pure love that comes from God. God, being the Creator, is an infinite being and as such must be infinite positive energy. That is why we feel such an amazing positive overflowing joy when we are in the presence of God.

Every person has a soul. In essence, we are a spiritual being in a physical body. We are all connected to God who is the source of our peace. Because our souls are connected to God, we feel a greater sense of peace and purpose when we spend more time with Him. When we are filled with the Holy Spirit, then we are much more likely to remain positive and joyous, no matter what our circumstances may be like.

Chapter 7 – The Importance of Positivity

What I am trying to do here is to show you that you are affected not only by your own state of mind, but also by other people's state of mind. When you are in a positive state of mind and you come in contact with a negative state of mind, then you immediately feel a conflict within yourself. We need to understand that a state of mind has the ability to affect other people's state of mind. When we look at a coal-fired Power Station, coal is burned, releasing its energy in the form of heat, which in turn heats up water to the point that it turns into steam. This high-pressure steam then transfers its energy to a turbine that turns a generator that turns it into electrical energy. This electrical energy is then transported to your home, where you use it with some appliance that turns it back into a different kind of energy. This example shows how the potential that is within one object can be accessed and transferred into a useful product to create a desired effect in another object.

In this same way, we connect with the world and either draw positivity or negativity from it, or give positivity or negativity into it, not as a measurable force, but more of an effect on emotion.

I have sometimes experienced a clear effect on my emotional energy levels depending on where I walk into. I have felt an immense positive influence on my emotions when walking into a church, and I have also felt a huge negative influence on my emotional energy when walking into some workplaces or homes. I believe this is because every person has the ability to affect the emotional energy of those around them and we have the ability to sense that change.

Chapter 7 – The Importance of Positivity

I have some distant family that are constantly fighting, and whenever we would go and visit, I would feel that negative effect on my emotions immediately when I walked into their house. I cannot imagine what it must be like to grow up in such an environment. Unfortunately, so many people do grow up in these environments, including their poor children. Remember earlier in the book where I spoke about how certain situations in your childhood could have an effect on you, even well into adulthood? This is one such situation. These children will grow up thinking that it is normal to feel anxious the whole time, or that it's OK for a husband and a wife to fight all the time or just avoid each other without speaking a word for days and even weeks at a time. As adults, we have the option of removing ourselves from situations like that, but children are not so lucky.

Let me share a story with you that one of my mentors, Mike Rodriguez shared with me. There was once a boy who lived in a small town. One day a circus came to town. The boy was very excited because he heard a lot about the amazing circus and their big tent. At the site where they were busy setting up the tent, the boy watched with wonder at how the big elephant was carrying the big poles and pulling the ropes with his strong trunk. The elephant was so strong, he could lift all the big poles of the tent with ease. Once the tent was completely set up and all the work was done, the elephant handler took the elephant off to one side where there was some grass and leaves for it to eat. He took a wooden stake and hit it into the ground. Then he proceeded to tie a rope around the elephant's leg and tied the other end to the wooden stake.

Chapter 7 – The Importance of Positivity

Then the elephant handler walked away, leaving the elephant all alone. When the little boy saw this, he ran to the handler shouting, "Wait, wait!" When he got to the handler he said, "Sir, you have made a big mistake. The elephant is too strong. He will easily break that piece of rope." The handler answered the boy and said, "You are right, the elephant is very strong, and he is surely strong enough to easily break the rope, but the elephant does not believe that he can break the rope." The boy was confused and he asked the handler what he meant. The handler told the boy that when the elephant was still very young, he used to tie it in exactly the same way. When the elephant was small, however, he was not strong enough to break free from the rope. No matter how hard he would pull, he could not break it. Eventually, the elephant believed that it was impossible to break the rope and stopped trying to break it altogether. That is why, even today, when he is strong enough to break it, he still believes that he isn't strong enough and doesn't even try.

You see, just like the elephant, some people get so conditioned during their childhood that they don't realize they can do something about it. They stay in bad situations in their adulthood because they became conditioned during their childhood that it is normal to live that way. People stay in abusive relationships, physical and emotional, thinking that it is normal. They are not happy but they think that is what it should be like. If you know someone like that, then it's up to you to help them. If you are living like that yourself, then it is time for you to change.

Chapter 7 – The Importance of Positivity

When you fall into a fire, you immediately realize that you must get out of the fire. Once you are out of the fire, you can focus on the stop, drop, and roll method to make sure you are not still on fire. Once that is done, you can focus on the burns and what you can do to heal them. You don't stop drop and roll while still in the fire. In the same way, you need to get out of the bad situation, then focus on getting rid of all the negativity by doing a spiritual "stop, drop, and roll." Then, once you have shaken all the negative influences, you can start healing by putting a wound dressing of positive influence on all your emotional burn wounds.

Positive influence can have an incredibly powerful effect on your life. By focusing on constantly immersing yourself in positive environments, you program your subconscious mind to always look for the positive. By always looking for the positive you will find it all around you.

When I was a young boy, we lived on a small mining village surrounded by a eucalyptus forest. I loved spending time in the forest. I felt so at peace and could spend hours and hours alone, without a care in the world. I loved watching the trees sway in the wind, the birds flying around, and listening to all the sounds of the forest. What I did not realize then was that the forest had a positive influence of its own, and by me spending time in the forest I was picking up on God's Spirit surrounding me as I spent time in the forest. This is what had such an amazing calming effect on me. As I grew more spiritually, I realized that God is in everything and that everything, especially nature, resonates with the Spirit of God. Now God's Spirit can't be measured, but when you are

Chapter 7 – The Importance of Positivity

closely connected to Him, then you can feel it. That is why people feel so close to God when in nature.

We need to understand that because God is the Creator of everything, He has a connection with everything and we need to be at peace with all of it. We can never reach our full potential if we treat animals badly. We cannot abuse part of God's creation and expect to feel at peace and live an abundant life.

"For in him all things were created: things in heaven and on earth, visible and invisible, whether thrones or powers or rulers or authorities; all things have been created through him and for him. He is before all things, and in him all things hold together." Colossians 1:16-17

At one of his training events that I attended, T. Harv Eker said that everything is energy, and energy is everything. That means that if you enthusiastically go after something and you keep up high positive energy, then you are much more likely to achieve success than if you were to go after that same goal with low energy. Get your energy up and go after your dreams.

Method 6 – Keep your mindset positive!
The fact is that our words have a direct impact on other living beings, and as such we need to be careful with our words. "The tongue has the power of life and death, and those who love it will eat its fruit." Proverbs 18:21

Chapter 7 – The Importance of Positivity

Now that you know the importance of your mindset and words, you can understand why you need to be vigilant about who you spend time with and also where you spend your time. Avoid places that are frequented by people with negative mindsets, places like bars, casinos, gentleman's clubs, or some dance clubs. The people that go there are usually filled with negativity and they are trying to find some joy in the wrong places. You need to find and spend time at places where people with positive mindsets tend to go. Places like self-development seminars and church.

Remember that God is light, and because the light of God also lives inside you, when you keep a positive mindset and increase your connection with God, then your light shines brighter. When a light is switched on in a dark room, then the darkness goes away. Darkness cannot exist in the light, which means that no evil can come close to you, or exist in the same space as you as long as you are connected to The Light, because then you are also a light to the world. (John 8:12)

Seek out positivity like it is a diamond that fell on your lawn. I can guarantee that you will keep looking until you find it. I know, because when I was eight years old my sister's gold filling was knocked loose from her tooth and fell on our lawn while we were playing tag. I searched relentlessly until I found it. Now if an eight-year-old can find a piece of gold the size of the tip of a pen on a lawn, then you can surely find positivity in this world. If you still struggle finding some, I suggest you go to the source of all positivity in all the universe:

Chapter 7 – The Importance of Positivity

Go to God!

Chapter 8 – Connecting with God

Chapter 8

Connecting with God

There had been times in my life when I had a lot of success and a lot of money, and there were times in my life when I barely made ends meet. Then there were times in my life when I was close to God, and really had a strong connection with Him, and there were times when I was distant from Him. Many times, these periods in my life overlapped, and I can tell you that those times when I was close to God I always felt much better than those times that I was distant from Him. Regardless of my financial position, God always had a major positive effect on me.

One day while I was engrossed in conversation with one of my friends, an image popped into my head of a giant oak tree. The image was not just like a still picture of a tree, it was almost like a slow-motion movie. Imagine the tree they showed in the movie Avatar. It wasn't that tree, but it had similarities. Let me explain. My vision was of a huge oak tree, but I could see the earth or soil it was planted in and I could see the roots. I could see the entire tree from root to tip, and it was a sectioned view like it was cut in half. I saw the life force energy moving from the soil into the roots, then traveling up the roots to the tree trunk, then following every

Chapter 8 – Connecting with God

branch to every single leaf. I saw the life cycle, if you will, of the tree. I saw new leaves forming while others were perfectly healthy and fully developed, and there were leaves turning and some leaves were falling from the tree to the soil below. Those leaves falling on the soil would then decompose, releasing its life force back into the soil. This energy was then renewed by the soil and sent back into the roots.

As this slow-motion movie was playing in my mind, I got the strong realization that that is what the world is like. The entire world is a massive oak tree, and we all are the leaves. God is the earth or soil and the tree is rooted within Him. God's energy would flow into the world, into every area of the world, and into every single living being on this planet. God would continue feeding his perfect love and energy into this tree and we (the leaves) would continue to live our lives from birth (the new leaves) to adulthood (fully formed leaves) to old age (the autumn leaves) to death (the falling leaves). Then we would return to God and we would become part of the entire ecosystem. Our life force energy, or soul, would live on and within this grand design of God, would keep contributing to the world.

We are so incredibly important to God's design, and it is time we learned that.

Ever since God created humans and placed them in the Garden of Eden, He wanted to have a relationship with us. That is why he would spend time with Adam and Eve in the garden. God wants us to be close to Him, because He loves

Chapter 8 – Connecting with God

us. It was our own weakness and giving in to deception that led to our sin. Ever since then, humans have struggled with sin and try to stay away from it.

God realized that He needed to help us to find freedom from condemnation. You see, the devil wants you to feel guilty about all your mistakes and sins, because if he can succeed in making you feel guilty about your sins and start to devalue yourself, then he has the ability to make you believe that you are not good enough for God, and that God doesn't love you. The truth is that God loves you very much, and because He loves you very much, He decided to do something to show you exactly how much. God sent His only Son, Jesus Christ to come and live as a man on this planet earth and ultimately give His life for us. (John 3:17)

Why did Jesus have to come to earth and live as a man to do this? The answer is because God needed someone completely righteous to die for our sins. Jesus had to live like a man, and be exposed to everything that we are exposed to. Jesus were tempted by the devil and the same stuff that we are tempted by, yet, He stayed pure and righteous. (Hebrews 4:15) Jesus never did anything wrong, yet, the people wanted Him dead. This was all part of God's grand plan. You see, Jesus was here not only to die for those that liked Him and listened to Him. He died for every single person on the face of this earth, those who were, who are, and are still to come. (1 Timothy 2:6) He died for those very people that were killing Him. Then He died and rose from the dead three days later, completely breaking the hold that death tried to have on him.

Chapter 8 – Connecting with God

Because of the sacrifice Jesus made for every single one of us, we are now free from condemnation and the law is fulfilled.

What does it mean to be free from condemnation?
It means that regardless of what you have done wrong in your life, and how much the devil wants to make you feel bad about it, Jesus says that you are washed clean by his sacrifice, because he already paid the price that you had to pay. (Hebrews 9:14) You see, Jesus was innocent from all sin. He was completely righteous, yet he took all our sins upon Himself and paid the ultimate sacrifice by giving up his life. It means that your sins have already been paid for, if you accept it. (Romans 10:9)

By accepting that Jesus paid the price for all your sins, you realize that you are clean and pure in the eyes of God, because of the blood of Jesus. You do not have to feel guilty anymore for anything you did in the past, because you have been washed completely clean. The devil doesn't want you to know this, because once you realize this, he no longer has any hold on you, and he hates it.

Now that you have been washed clean from your past, you need to live a life that reflects that. (Philippians 1:27; Colossians 1:9-14) It is like hitting the reset button and being able to start over. How many times have you wished that you could go back in time and do things differently, be a better person or undo some wrongs? This is like that. The freedom of the blood of Jesus is not a free pass to keep sinning, though. (Romans 6:1-2; 1 John 3:6)

Chapter 8 – Connecting with God

It is a chance to do better, to be better, and to live a more righteous life, just like Jesus did. The law being fulfilled means that we can now focus on having a relationship with God and stop trying to earn our place in heaven by fulfilling the acts of the law from the first testament.

"But if we walk in the light as He is in the light, we have fellowship with one another, and the blood of Jesus Christ His Son cleanses us from all sin." 1 John 1:7 (NKJV)

The most wonderful thing about accepting that Jesus died for you and that you are now clean is the fact that you can pray with freedom and confidence. (Hebrews 4:16) You can speak to God as your Father. If you are weighed down with guilt and condemnation, it is very difficult, impossible even, to have an open relationship with God. Why? Because you don't feel like you are good enough. You don't feel you are worthy of His love, and hence, when you ask for things in prayer, you never believe that you will get them, because you don't believe that you deserve it. Because he makes you clean and free from condemnation, you can come before your Father in heaven and ask Him with confidence and love, and just as a good father likes to give good gifts to his son, so too does God like and want to give you good gifts.

"If you, then, though you are evil, know how to give good gifts to your children, how much more will your Father in heaven give good gifts to those who ask him!" Matthew 7:11 (NIV)

Chapter 8 – Connecting with God

God wants to give you good gifts when you ask it with a pure heart and pure intentions. (James 4:3)

In Mark 11:24 it is written, "Therefore I tell you, whatever you ask for in prayer, believe that you have received it, and it will be yours." And in Psalm 37:4 it is written, "Take delight in the LORD, and He will give you the desires of your heart." These Scriptures tell us that if we ask for something we will receive it, but as I said before, your intention needs to be pure.

I believe that when you have a close relationship with God, then the desires of your heart change. He will give us the desires we should have. You no longer ask for prideful things for prideful reasons, but you ask with pure intentions.

Here is an example: Before you had a great relationship with God, you might have asked for a new SUV because you really wanted to look good and show off, but when your intentions are pure you might ask for a new Mercedes-Benz minibus because you want to be able to drive more people to and from work, or to church, or to take some foster children to the zoo or the aquarium. You see, there is nothing wrong with wanting a new vehicle, even a top of the line one. What matters is your intention. Now that does not mean that you cannot have a nice SUV. If God wants to bless you with one, then He will surely give it to you, but it should never take a bigger place than God in your life. Don't let pride or ego or self-obsession drive you away from God.

Chapter 8 – Connecting with God

Having a relationship with God, Jesus, and the Holy Spirit is such a blessing. When Jesus went back to Heaven to be with God, the Holy Spirit was sent down so each one of us could always have someone with us. That way, we would never be lonely. It is like having a part of God's consciousness with us every second of the day. (John 14:16-18, 16:7)

That means that we can have conversations with Him the entire day and we can share our hopes and dreams with Him. In fact, He wants us to, because He placed those dreams inside of you. You can talk to Him when you are sad, when you are angry, and when you feel frustrated. No longer do you need to suffer through your emotions, but you can give them to God. You can give all your problems to God. He knows what to do with them. (1 Peter 5:7; Matthew 11:28-30)

Remember that all those dreams that you have in your heart were placed there. Martin Luther King Jr. once famously gave his "I have a dream" speech. He had a vision and a dream, but in truth, that dream had a hold of him. It was placed inside of him by God. In the same way, all of us have dreams placed within all of us. The question is whether or not we have enough courage to go after our dreams. Do we have enough courage to chase after our dreams when everyone else is telling us that it is a silly dream? When the whole world is against us, are we willing to keep going? You might not think that you have what it takes to pursue your dreams. You might be telling yourself that your dreams are too big for you and that you will never be able to achieve it. You doubt yourself, and you are afraid that you might not

Chapter 8 – Connecting with God

make it. The short answer is that by yourself, you cannot. But that dream was placed inside your heart by God, and with His help, you can do anything. You can achieve whatever you set your mind to. Trust that when God has given you a dream, that He will also give you the skills and abilities to achieve it. He will also give you the resources to achieve it. (2 Timothy 3:17) God will bring the people that can help you, the skills you need to learn, and whatever you may need. You just need to trust Him.

Don't try to go through life alone. The Holy Spirit is always with you. All you need to do is be quiet and pray, and give all your problems to God. (Psalm 46:10) Prayer is like your direct call line with God Himself. Sometimes it might feel like a one-sided conversation, but I promise you that God hears every word and He knows your heart. Just trust Him. If you want to have a proper view of all the hurt and pain from your past, all the feelings of inferiority and rejection, then I suggest delving into a deeper relationship with God, and if you never had a relationship with Him, then start one. Invite Jesus into your life by accepting what He did for you, knowing that all your sins are forgiven. (Ephesians 1:7; Colossians 1:13-14) You can now have full on, mind altering, heart transformational love and relationship with your Creator. (2 Corinthians 5:17) Nothing, no person, or job, or business, or any amount of money will ever be able to replace the place of God.

To truly have a relationship with God you need to spend time working at it like any other relationship. You need to spend as much time as you can learning about Him. You can

Chapter 8 – Connecting with God

do this by reading about Him and by spending time talking about Him with others so you can grow spiritually. If people spend years studying to finish school and get a degree, then we can all spend more time studying God.

You need to spend time in conversation with Him. As I said earlier, the freedom that you were given from the blood of Jesus, has given you an open line to speak to God. Spend as much time as you can in conversation with Him through prayer.

Learn to listen, not to people, but to God. As your relationship with Him grows, your hearing will improve, and you will hear God's voice. Throughout the bible there are a few places where it mentions God speaking, but it is mostly a whisper in the wind, a quiet voice, and if you want to hear it, you need to be still and learn to listen. You need to have unwavering faith. We think that we understand what faith is. In truth, it is a belief that something will in fact happen, even when all the odds are stacked against it. Having unwavering faith means to keep believing, even when it makes absolute no sense at all, and no one and nothing will stop you from believing it. Believe that God knows what is best for you and that He will bring it to pass when you are ready. Remember that power has corrupted many people, and he wants to be sure that you are ready to handle it. Leap like a three-year-old into the arms of your Daddy and trust that He will catch you.

Respect the Lord. That means keeping His commandments and doing what He tells you when He speaks to you.

Chapter 8 – Connecting with God

Remember that it will not always be something that you want to do, but you still need to do it. Remember that in the Bible, Jonah did not want to go to his enemies in Nineveh, as God commanded him to do. Jonah wanted them to be destroyed and tried to run away. Eventually, God had to send a fish to swallow him before he would listen. Learn to listen to God and respect His wishes. No one deserves your respect more than God does. Also, live a life that is worthy of God's respect.

Praise. There are few things that God loves more than praise. Spend time every day praising God. Sing at the top of your lungs, sing whatever comes to mind, sing even when the words make no sense. God understands and he knows your heart. I sing and praise God all the time, mostly when I am driving and I am alone in the car. I would sing in different languages, that I did not understand. Some call it speaking in tongues. Well, I would sing in tongues. Every time I did this, I would feel the presence of God, and I would get goose bumps all over. Afterwards, the devil would always try to doubt that what I sang was for the Lord. Since it was a language I could not understand, it is sometimes easy for the doubt to creep in. One day I went to a Christian conference where a great preacher was speaking. He was a very humble man, with a great connection with God. Throughout the event he would give messages to people in the room. Answers to prayers, if you will. Then, in the second part of his talk, he walked in my direction, looked right in my eyes, and asked my name. Then he told me that God loves my singing, and that even though I don't understand it, God thinks it is beautiful.

Chapter 8 – Connecting with God

He said that my songs were strong spiritual warfare songs. I was completely blown away, because I had never told anybody about the singing; nobody knew except for God, and this was a direct confirmation from God that he loved my singing. I knew that there was no way that the preacher could have known about my singing if it was not for God telling him.

Just like with me, God hears you, and He loves it when you praise Him, so spend time praising and glorifying Him. Speak about Him. Don't be afraid to speak about God, and about the wonderful work that Jesus completed. There are millions of people all over the world that are lost and do not know what Jesus did to set them free. They do not know that they have a Father in Heaven who is longing for a relationship with them, who loves them regardless of whatever they might have done. Feel free to speak to people about what the Lord has done in your life. People might try to argue with what you believe or say, but they will never be able to argue with the evidence of the miracle works of God in your life. Give your life, career, marriage, children, finances, business, everything over to God, and see what amazing things He can do with it. There is nothing in this world that we can do better than He who created us. If you truly want to see the full significance of your life like I know you do, then align yourself with God's purpose for you. The feeling of His love and acceptance is the best feeling in the world. You've got nothing to lose and everything to gain. Go ahead and let God in!

Method 7 – Really connect with God daily.

Chapter 8 – Connecting with God

Chapter 9

The Significance of Reward

Every human on the face of the earth is motivated by something. That motivation is a strong drive that makes them pursue a given task with vigor and determination. Motivation alone will never be enough unless there is a reward waiting for you at the end. Those rewards can come in many different shapes and sizes.

When you are a newborn baby, for example, you have a very important goal. That goal is to be fed and you are motivated by your growling stomach. Your only available option at this age to get your hungry belly filled is to scream as hard as you can until someone comes and feeds you. If no one comes, you keep screaming, louder and more emotionally, still motivated by the growl of nothingness in your stomach. If you persist in your endeavors, then finally someone comes along and gives you the reward for all your hard work in the form of milk that satisfies your hunger.

When you are an adult and you get hungry, then you have the same ultimate goal, but your method of going after your

Chapter 9 – The Significance of Reward

goal will be different from that of a baby. You can try lying around and screaming and crying for someone to feed you, but I can say with almost one hundred percent certainty that people will only think you are crazy and you will go to sleep hungry. As an adult, you can choose what you want to eat, and you can plan the entire process, from the route you are going to the restaurant, whether to take the bus, a taxi, or the subway, or if you are going to walk. The reward is the same in both scenarios, but the method of achieving it is completely different.

There are many different rewards. It might be a new job, a new car, a new house, an ice cream, or a concert ticket, to name only a few. Even when you started dating the ultimate end goal, or reward if you will, was a husband or a wife. All of the things between when you started dating in the first place, right up until you met your soulmate, were still in pursuit of the reward.

One of the biggest problems in the world today is that people get confused about what exactly the reward is. Many people think that money is a reward. When they focus so much on getting more money, they forget what they really want to accomplish. Once they get a lot of money, they realize that they still feel empty and that they did not achieve anything, and this makes them unhappy. They think that getting even more money is the answer, and the vicious cycle continues. Money is a tool. The main purpose of money is to be able to purchase our rewards for hard work. You see, getting money at the end of the month or a big bonus at the end of the year, is not a reward. What you spend it on is your reward.

Chapter 9 – The Significance of Reward

You cannot eat your money, but you can buy food, which is a reward to your body for working so hard. You want to give it good nutrition in order for it to stay strong. When you have worked very hard all year long, you get that bonus. The bonus isn't the reward, but the nice vacation you take your family on is the reward. The vacation is also a reward for your family for supporting you while you were working so hard all year long. There has to be a reward for your actions. If you don't clearly define your reward for your actions, then you will quickly get discouraged and lose hope.

Unfortunately, money has gotten a bad rap over the years, and people say that money is the root of all evil, when in fact, it is not money itself, but the love of it that is the root of evil. Note that the Scripture does not say the love of money is evil, it says it is the root of evil. It all depends on what you are doing with it. (1 Timothy 6:10) When you love money to the point that you value it more than you value God, or your family, or your friends, or even human or animal life, then it becomes evil. Again, it is not the money itself that is evil, but what you would do to get it or what you spend it on that can be evil.

In Africa, rhinos are being poached at an alarming rate and the horns are sold for ridiculous amounts of money because some cultures believe that it has special abilities to enhance male performance. Because of their vain reasons for wanting the horns and willingness to pay high sums of money for it, these poor animals are hunted to the verge of extinction. It is not the money in and of itself that is evil, but what the people are willing to do to get it that is evil.

Chapter 9 – The Significance of Reward

Money is a magnifier; if you are a good person and you get a lot of money, then you will be a better person. Why? Because good people tend to go out of their way to help others, and if you have more money, then you will invariably help more people. The flipside is that if you are a bad person and get lots of money, then you will be an even worse person. Just look at some of the dictators around the world, especially in Africa. They will steal, plunder, and destroy in order to stay in power and to get more money. Robert Mugabe has destroyed Zimbabwe's economy and refuses to relinquish power to someone else as was evident through the 2008 elections. He lives a lavish lifestyle, traveling the world in luxury, while the citizens of the country hardly have enough food to eat. The currency had descended into a devastating abyss, causing the people to suffer even more. I am not saying that Robert Mugabe was not a good leader in his prime, but what happened in Zimbabwe can be seen as a good example of what happens when a leader becomes power hungry and refuses to let other better suited leaders take over to the detriment of the economy. Along these lines, drug cartels from around the world will do just about anything to make more money.

You see, money is not the problem. It is the people that use it that is the problem. This leads me to my next point. If we are good people and we walk around saying money is bad and that we don't want to have a lot of it, because it will make us evil, then what we are doing is leaving it all in the hands of the drug dealers, war lords, and dictators. I can guarantee you that they do not have any good planned with it.

Chapter 9 – The Significance of Reward

Don't be afraid of money and don't be ashamed of having a lot of it. Make as much of it as you can, then use it to do a lot of good. Imagine that you walk into a store and you buy yourself a soda. Now, just say for argument's sake that Bill Gates is in the same store buying the same soda. Is there any difference to the value of the item that you both bought? The answer is no.

The value of the money that we have is exactly the same as the value of the money of the wealthy. The wealthy just have more of it. What we spend our money on has a far greater effect on the amount of money we end up with than we would like to admit. The poor tend to spend their money on non-value adding stuff like cars, takeout meals, movies, fancy phones, and unnecessary luxuries, while the wealthy tend to spend their money on value adding items like personal development, books, audio programs, investments, and businesses. This leads to the same conundrum of the chicken and the egg. Do they spend their money on those things because they are wealthy, or are they wealthy because they spend their money on those things? The same can be asked of poor people. Do they not spend money on personal development or growth because they can't afford it, or are they poor because they don't spend their money on personal development?

Many times, people with a poor mindset might say that they can't afford to go to a seminar or buy a book, but then pay more on concert tickets or tickets to the movies. No matter how hard we try to fight the facts, we are in the positions we

Chapter 9 – The Significance of Reward

are because of the choices we make, the actions we take, and because of what we spend our money on. If you are unhappy with your life at this moment, then ask yourself this question, "What have I been spending my money and time on?" Be honest with yourself and it will give you a good picture of your priorities and what you need to change in order to change your direction in life. Don't wait until it is too late. Start today, and you can end up in a completely different place from where you are today. Remember that money is only a tool and this tool can be used to purchase rewards.

Be clear about what your rewards are and when exactly you will get the reward. Make sure that you are specific and never reward bad habits. That would be like giving sweets to a child who is throwing a tantrum. It reinforces the bad behavior. Don't do that to yourself. Be strict, but be fair.

Method 8 – Reward yourself.
When you sit down to do your goal setting, (and if you haven't done that then you need to do it) make sure that every goal has a clear reward attached to it. Never leave a goal without a reward.

Just like you have small rewards for every aspect of your life, it is also important to have an ultimate goal for your life. What is it that you want to achieve? What is it that you want to be remembered for? What will your legacy be? I know what mine is. It is to have an impact on the world, to be known as a good man, a good husband and father, a good friend, and a kind-hearted man that always treated everyone with respect and love.

Chapter 9 – The Significance of Reward

My ultimate reward for living this life is to one day hear God say the words, "Well done good and faithful servant." Just imagine hearing your Heavenly Father saying "Well done" and that He is proud of you. That must be the most amazing reward in the universe.

I sincerely hope that you also get to hear those words one day!

Chapter 9 – The Significance of Reward

Chapter 10

Living a Significant Life

Throughout this book, you have learned how valuable you are just as you are. You have learned that you are indeed significant. Now the next question that comes up is, "How do I live a significant life?"

In this chapter we will focus on a few different concepts that will help you to understand how to live a significant life. Living a significant life will mean different things to different people and you need to determine exactly what it means to you.

I always love to share a story of what happened with me a couple of years ago. I was twenty-seven years old and I was working as a maintenance boilermaker at a very large stainless steel smelter in South Africa. It was a time in my life when I was just starting to walk a more intimate journey with God. You see, I had realized one day, while upset, that I was in the habit of cussing quite badly. One of the supervisors laughed and said, "Well it didn't take you long to fit in." That just puts it into perspective that most of the guys in the unit cussed a lot. His words had a profound impact on me and I

Chapter 10 – Living a Significant Life

realized right there that that is not the type of person I wanted to be, that is not who I want to be known as. I didn't want to be the foul-mouthed boilermaker in the plant. I decided right there that I was going to make a change. Slowly but surely, I started to cuss less. Every time I would catch myself wanting to say something, I would just stop. Once I made a conscious choice to focus on stopping, I suddenly became more aware of my words. Eventually, I completely transformed my vocabulary. Cussing was just no longer part of it. As time went by, I kept it that way. One day as we were sitting in the tearoom, some of the other artisans were cracking jokes just like they usually did, nothing bad, just joking and laughing. One of the gentleman said a cuss word and immediately apologized to me. When I asked him why he was apologizing, he said because he cussed in front of me, and that he didn't want to. When I asked why, he replied that when he was with me, he felt like he wanted to be better. You see, I never, not once, made any comment to any of the other people at work about their language. I only focused on myself and making myself a better person, and in the process, I helped another person realize that he also wanted to be better.

That is just one story of how your actions can make a huge difference in the world. Your thoughts can also have a major impact not only on your own life, but also on those around you. (2 Corinthians 10:5) Now you might be thinking, why would my thoughts have an effect on other people? It is because the way you think about other people affects how you see them. When you think badly about them, then you probably do not make any effort to speak with them.

Chapter 10 – Living a Significant Life

As I discussed earlier in this book, it is very important to focus on filling your mind with positive self-talk, but remember to fill it with positive talk about others as well. (Philippians 2:3-4)

Next, you need to learn how to give.
In 2 Corinthians 9:7 it is written, "Each of you should give what you have decided in your heart to give, not reluctantly or under compulsion, for God loves a cheerful giver." We need to be cheerful givers. We should not give begrudgingly or full of disdain. We need to open our hearts and share our blessings.

Now, we all know this, but it is not necessarily so easy to do. Unfortunately, there are always a few bad apples that spoil it for everyone else. Some people want to suck you dry and just never know when to stop. My wife has a nice quote that says, "The giver needs to stop giving, because the taker will never stop taking." In many cases that is true, but I also believe that we should learn to give as we feel led. Now don't go around never giving and hide your stinginess behind not feeling led to do so. I believe that it is important to ask God to show you when He wants you to help someone or bless them. You see, helping can be in actions or financially. Giving can be through a loan to help someone through a tough time. Blessing someone is when you feel led to give someone something, no strings attached. Make sure you cut those strings. You can't walk around with strings attached to every person you ever helped just waiting for the opportunity to yank on those strings when you need them to do something for you.

Chapter 10 – Living a Significant Life

Never allow someone to take advantage of you and stop you from helping others.

I was driving home one day with my small, little car. As I drove into town, I saw a family standing under a tree and the dad was hitchhiking. It was a husband and a wife, five children, and a bunch of bags. Initially, I drove past them. There was no way all of them would have fit in my small, little car. As I kept going right past them, I felt compelled to stop and help them. I did not know how I was going to help them, but I knew I had to try. I drove around the block and stopped next to them. It turns out that the father just got a new job in a city 400 miles away. His new boss bought him a bus ticket and arranged accommodation for his family at a resort a few miles out of town. They had been trying to get a ride to the bus station for him to catch the bus, but nobody would stop. There was only eighteen minutes before the bus arrived and the bus station was fifteen miles away. Luckily, another person stopped just behind me, also in a small car. We agreed that I would take the father to the bus stop, while the other person would take the rest of the family to the resort. They were bunched in, but they all fit, even though just barely. When I dropped off the father, we exchanged phone numbers and he went to catch the bus.

About a week later, he made contact with me again. This time, he asked me for a couple of bucks for food, since he had not received his first paycheck yet from his new job. Almost immediately I felt upset, feeling taken advantage off. I felt like I already went out of my way to help him and now he wanted more. I very nearly talked myself out of helping

Chapter 10 – Living a Significant Life

him again, but then I remembered in Luke 6:30 where it says to give to everyone who asks you. I didn't really want to at first, but I realized that I could never out-give God, so I sent him some cash.

Just like this event that happened to me, we will all have to deal with people that need help at some point in time. We all have a journey to walk, and we all have a difference to make in this world. At one point, my wife and I were talking about that event, and I commented about how so many people drove right by them, some with vehicles big enough to fit the entire family, but they never stopped. My wife made a very powerful statement that day. You see, I was judging them for not stopping, but my wife made me realize that it was not necessarily placed on their hearts to stop. It was placed on mine.

God will speak to you, when he wants you to help someone; you just need to be obedient.

Be a good teacher. Throughout your life, you will learn many things, some from school, others from experience. You will end up with a treasure chest of knowledge. The most important thing you can do with your treasure is to share it. Most people try to keep their knowledge and experience all to themselves because they are afraid that someone might steal their thunder, or overshadow them, or steal their job. Instead of being afraid, share freely, take someone under your wing, and teach them everything you know. Watch them soar, knowing that you had a major impact on their lives.

Chapter 10 – Living a Significant Life

Be a good listener. There are many people in the world who feel that they are drowning, feeling lost and upset. These people have an immense desire to be loved and heard. By spending time just listening to other people, you have the ability to make them feel like their story is important and that you value them enough to give them some of your time and attention. To some, it might be the only form of acceptance they have ever gotten. Since you won't always know every person's backstory, it is safe to assume that they all just need some love and attention. I have never met any person that ever said, "Stop, stop, enough already, I can't deal with all the love, it is just too much, please don't love me so much." That just won't happen. People love feeling loved and valued.

Be kind to children. Children are very vulnerable, their emotions are not yet fully developed yet, and they get hurt easily. We might think that they do not, because of the brave face they might put on, but they get hurt easily. Children are also brilliant at adapting and if they realize that they are being abused physically or emotionally, they will tend to climb into a shell. They try not to attract any unnecessary attention to themselves in the hope that they might avoid the abuse. Be kind to them by treating them with love and care. Tell them they are awesome every single day, more than once. Who doesn't like to hear they are awesome? Teach them new stuff every day and never think that they are too young to understand. I told my son when he was still four-years-old, step by step, exactly how an internal combustion engine works. Why? Because he asked me, and I knew. I didn't want to lie to him by saying 'I don't know' just to avoid trying to

Chapter 10 – Living a Significant Life

explain it to him, because I wanted to avoid all the "but why's." When he was two-years-old, he already knew the entire water evaporation cycle. He asked where the water went when we pulled the plug from the bathtub and I told him.

Never, ever think that they are too young to understand. When he asks me about something that he is still a little too young to know, then I tell him that he is a little too young and I give him the age that he must be for me to tell him. That way, he knows exactly where we stand, and he knows that he will get his answer in the future.

Be kind to the elderly. I sometimes feel so bad when I walk into an old age home and I see the old people sitting around. Some of them seem so lonely. They lived a full life, they learned so much, they have so much knowledge, but everyone treats them like children. Sometimes they feel like the world has forgotten them. If you spend some time chatting with them, let them teach you some of their knowledge. They have a huge hard drive full of knowledge, just waiting to be downloaded into someone willing to accept it. It is sad that many of the elderly in old age homes live in conditions that are worse than convicts in some prisons. That is just appalling and is something that needs to be addressed.

Be kind to animals. Animals can be so loving and caring, and they are just like family. Even animals that we thought could never be domesticated can be caring and loving in the right

Chapter 10 – Living a Significant Life

circumstances. Even lions can act like little docile house cats when they are raised that way.

Don't be cruel to animals. No animal deserves to be abused or neglected.

Smile! There is nothing more beautiful to me than a person who smiles. When a smile is real and sincere, you can see it in the eyes. The eyes light up and it is almost as if you can see kindness flowing from them. It warms my heart and always puts a smile on my face as well. Do your best to always greet people with a smile. When you are walking on a street, look at people. Don't walk with your head down, looking at your phone the whole time. Look up, look the world in the eyes, and smile your biggest, most sincere smile that you can. I can guarantee you that most people will smile back, and you greet them with the same enthusiasm and sincerity. The world is already too full of glum people. Instead of blending into the crowd of faceless blobs, (because everyone is looking down at their phones) be a light that brightens up someone's day.

I can tell you that my wife has the most beautiful smile in the world, (OK, I'm biased) and that is one of the aspects that attracted me to her. Whenever I have a rough day and get home, the moment I see her beautiful smile all my cares just melt away.

Don't be afraid to share your beautiful smile.
Hug freely! There is an amazing power in that moment when someone gives you a sincere hug. When someone gives you

Chapter 10 – Living a Significant Life

a hug with no intention other than to show you compassion in the form of a physical embrace, it truly brings joy to your soul. Just like a smile, when a hug is sincere, you can feel it. Earlier in the book, we discussed how every living being is connected because we are all connected to our Creator. So when someone gives you a sincere hug, you can really sense the loving positive effect from the hug. A sincere hug has the power to make someone feel better or sometimes help them to let go of their emotions.

I have seen at funerals how a person would put on a brave face. The moment they get a sincere hug from someone that truly cares for them, they would just start crying. That is because they can feel the care from that person and the empathy they have for them. They feel safe enough to be vulnerable with that person. Be the type of person with whom others can be vulnerable. Show them that you truly care, and always be ready with a sincere hug. Remember that many people in the world have never felt the sincere embrace of a fellow human being, so share hugs freely! Be the kind of person that always brings hope to the world. Be positive, be inspiring, be joyful, be friendly, but most importantly, be you.

The title of this book is 'the significance of being born' because I sincerely hope that you begin to understand how incredibly important and significant you are to the world. Nothing and no one can take your place. You are one of a kind. You were not born to blend in, you were born to stand out. You were not created to hide away, you were created to shine like the beaming light of a lighthouse. Remember that

Chapter 10 – Living a Significant Life

you have the DNA of God inside of you and as such you are royalty. A child of the King of Kings. Don't diminish your value by listening to what the world says about you. The world today is full of people and companies that want you to feel inferior. They do this because they want to sell their products. Large corporate companies, especially fashion and cosmetics companies, want to make you feel ugly and overweight and that you are just not good enough the way you are in order for you to buy their product. Their selfish ambitions have destroyed more people's self-esteem than anything else in the world.

Let me tell you right now that you are beautiful and that you have a valuable place in this world! You just need to focus on finding it. The most important thing that you need to remember is that you are a spiritual being. Your body is just the vessel that carries your soul at this moment. Your looks, weight, hair color, eye color, or the shape of your nose has absolutely nothing to do with who you are inside. Let your beautiful soul shine brighter every day, and I can promise you, all those things you are self-conscious about will fade away.

Don't conform to this world. (Romans 12:2)
The unmistakable fact is that there are a lot of things in this world that are wrong. There is a lot of poverty, there is a lot of pain, and there is a lot of suffering. Most of that is because people have forgotten how to love their fellow human beings, regardless of where they come from, what they look like, what they wear, what they eat, what they drink, what they pray, what language they speak, or what the color of

Chapter 10 – Living a Significant Life

their skin is. Every single human life is significant! So remember to love everyone with the love that only God can give. In Luke 3:38, Luke describes Adam as the son of God. If we, then, are all descendants of Adam, then we are in fact descendants of God and we carry His DNA within every one of us. And if man is made in the image of God, as mentioned in Genesis 1:26, then we should not judge any man, because in essence you are then judging the handiwork of God. That's not what we're supposed to be doing.

People don't value their lives and because of their suffering and pain, they feel worthless. Because of this, they look for meaning in a bottle or in a needle or in a tablet. They try to find a sense of euphoria. They look for a high to numb their pain, to numb the way they feel because they like the way they feel when they experience that high. I know, because when I was a young man I used to drink a lot because I was very shy. That was my way of expressing myself, because when I was drunk I felt free. I didn't feel any inhibitions and I could be myself, but the fact was that afterwards I still felt alone. It wasn't until I started to develop myself that I could start to see my own worth. Then things started to change.

Remember that when people are in this destructive state of mind they easily lash out at those around them in very hurtful ways. This is not a reflection of you, but rather of where they are in their minds at that moment and you should not take anything they say personally. If you still find this difficult, then I suggest that you go back to chapter 5.

Chapter 10 – Living a Significant Life

You need to start to see yourself the way God intended you to be, and the way He still sees you every day. Nothing you have done can take away God's love from you. He renews you! He doesn't just clean you up a bit and wipe you off. He makes you brand-new! You need to start living up to your potential. You are magnificent! You are good enough, and you can do anything you set your mind to. Don't let anyone ever tell you otherwise.

Once you start to see a glimmer of the person you can be, you should hang onto that. You should grab onto it and hold on tightly and never let go until you see that picture more vividly every single day, until one day, that person looks back at you from the mirror. You can be whatever you set your mind on, because you were created that way, but by devaluing yourself and saying that you are not worth it, you will not be able to reach those goals.

You need to find yourself, you need to find your purpose, and you need to find your joy. You do not need to see exactly where you're going, just start and the path will present itself. Zig Ziglar once said, "Go as far as you can see, and when you get there you will see further." You don't need to see the entire road. When you take a journey, it doesn't matter if it is a 100 miles or 1,000 miles, you don't see the end destination when you start. In fact, you don't see the end destination until you are at the end, but you can see a couple of miles in front of you. When you're driving in heavy rain or dense fog, you can only see a couple of yards in front of you. But you will reach your destination. Focus on where you

Chapter 10 – Living a Significant Life

want to go, grab that image, hold it in your mind, and believe it. Trust that this is who you can be. Believe in yourself.

Believe in your potential, and you will be able to achieve it every day, a little bit at a time, and you will get there. If you focus on trying to be 1% better each day, then you will be completely different in one years' time, because the law of compound interest says that you will be more than 3000% better by just getting 1% better every day. You are meant for greatness. You might not believe it right now, but I'm telling you, it's true. For many years, I didn't believe in myself. I knew there was something more. I knew that I wanted to do something more, but I didn't know how and I didn't believe that I was capable. Even after I reached a lot of success, I still didn't believe in myself because I still hung onto my old way of thinking and my old habits. If you want to change your destination and you want to change your future, you need to let go of your old habits. You need to let go of your old way of thinking and you need to replace it with a brand-new way of thinking. You need to step up and live up to the person you were meant to be.

Don't stop when it gets difficult, because it will get difficult. I believe the difficulty is a way to weed out the weak, because the weak quit when it gets difficult. You are not weak. You are strong! You have the DNA of God Almighty within you. You are unstoppable. Nothing can stand in your way. Do not quit! It is impossible to beat someone that never quits. It doesn't matter how tough it gets, it doesn't matter how many times you fall and hit the ground, you get back up again, you go for it, you work, you fight, you bite, you sweat, you bleed,

Chapter 10 – Living a Significant Life

but you don't quit. (2 Corinthians 4:8-10) You keep going even when it seems that there is no way that you can do it.

You keep going and you will be successful. I promise you, if you do not quit, you will be successful. There were times in my life that I was completely broke, I had no hope, and I couldn't even imagine how I was going to get up. But I never quit and God always made a way. You need to focus your energy and your attention on making the best of every situation, no matter how bad it is. What is the lesson you can learn from every situation and how can you apply those lessons to your life to make better decisions next time?

As a royal child of the King of Kings, you have seeds of greatness within you! Don't settle for mediocrity, don't settle for just getting by, day by day, barely making a living, barely surviving. Do something more. Why don't you go out and try something you have never done before? Surprise yourself. Rise up and be different. Make a difference in the world and change people's lives. Treat them with respect and value them and they will love you, and even when they don't, you still treat them with love and respect, because that is who you are. Bring glory to God through everything that you do. You don't allow your world to descend into anarchy if somebody doesn't agree with you. You live up to your full potential. "Be the change you want to see in the world."
– Ghandi

Remember that many people in the world do not know God. Part of our purpose is to live a life that reflects God to the

Chapter 10 – Living a Significant Life

world. Through your faithful actions, other people should be able to see God's love in action.

"Life: it's not about brilliance, it's not about reputation, it's about making a difference."
- Pieter Van Der Westhuizen

Thank you!

Chapter 10 – Living a Significant Life

Chapter 10 – Living a Significant Life

The Significance of Being Born

About the Author

Pieter Van Der Westhuizen was born as the youngest of five children in a small mining village near Witbank on the Highveld of Mpumalanga, South Africa. Pieter grew up as a very shy boy and because of his shyness, he always felt like he struggled to fit in. Pieter, however, loved the outdoors and spent most of his spare time in the forest surrounding the village. He spent many years teaching himself how to overcome his shyness. This led to many achievements throughout his life. By the age of 34, Pieter had worked as a Boilermaker Artisan for more than 12 years, as a project buyer and he has spent time in the military as command post assistant and radar operator in both the South African Army and Air Force. Pieter also holds a private pilot's license and is a licensed financial advisor.

After a devastating head-on car accident in September 2009, Pieter had to radically re-shape his life. Since then, he has become the first Ziglar Legacy Certified Trainer in Africa and has been involved with motivational speaking and coaching since 2012. Pieter has an incredible insight into what makes people function at their peak and he is very passionate about making a difference in the world, while helping others to achieve more. Pieter believes that with God all things are possible and he lives his life that way.

www.BreakingTheZone.com

The Significance of Being Born

The Significance of Being Born

Disclaimer & Copyright Information

Some of the events, locales, and conversations have been recreated from memories. In order to maintain their anonymity, in some instances, the names of individuals and places have been changed. As such, some identifying characteristics and details may have changed.

Although the author and publisher have made every effort to ensure that the information in this book was correct at press time, the author and publisher do not assume and hereby disclaim any liability to any party for any loss, damage, or disruption caused by errors or omissions, whether such errors or omissions result from negligence, accident, or any other cause.

All quotes, unless otherwise noted,
are attributed to the respective Author or to the Holy Bible.

Cover illustration, book design and production
Copyright © 2017 by Tribute Publishing, LLC
www.TributePublishing.com

Scripture references are copyrighted by www.BibleGateway.com which is operated by the Zondervan Corporation, L.L.C.

Citations:

1 Oakland University

2 www.iflscience.com/health-and-medicine/breast-milk-custom-formulated-baby's-gender/

The Significance of Being Born

The Significance of Being Born

The Significance of Being Born

The Significance of Being Born

NOTES

The Significance of Being Born

NOTES

www.ingramcontent.com/pod-product-compliance
Lightning Source LLC
Chambersburg PA
CBHW021130300426
44113CB00006B/363